The Kilkenny Incest Case

The KILKENNY INCEST CASE

As told to Kieron Wood

POOLBEG

The picture on the front cover is a school photograph of Alison, aged 9, taken the year before the abuse began.

First published 1993 by
Poolbeg
A Division of Poolbeg Enterprises Ltd,
Knocksedan House,
Swords, Co Dublin, Ireland.

© Kieron Wood and Alison Cooper 1993

A catalogue record for this book is available from the British Library.

ISBN 1 85371 189 6

Cover design by Poolbeg Press
Set by Mac Book Limited in Stone 11/15
Printed by Guernsey Press Limited,
Vale, Guernsey, Channel Islands.

To Arron and Serena

AUTHOR'S NOTE

The names of the main characters in this book have been changed to protect the privacy of the people involved. Nothing else has been changed.

The passages in italics at the beginning of Chapters 1-16 are taken verbatim from statements made by Alison Cooper to the gardai.

CONTENTS

FOREWORD

In my twenty-five years as a journalist, I've covered all sorts of major stories. But nothing I've ever done has had the impact of the story of Alison Cooper.

Her stark tale of sixteen years of horror gripped the Irish nation. The details she so graphically recounted in a television interview appalled everyone who heard them.

The day after the RTE news interview, the whole country was talking about it. It was the front page story in every national newspaper. Radio stations throughout Ireland were inundated with shocked callers. Questions were asked in the Dáil.

Ministers promised changes in the law and the promise was honoured. Within weeks, the maximum penalty for incest against a child over the age of fifteen was increased from seven to twenty years.

But it would be tragic if Alison's story were merely to become a political issue, with special interest groups using it to bolster their own agenda for political change.

The response to Alison's sufferings should not be a witchhunt, but a balanced and considered programme of changes to the law and proper funding for a range of improvements to facilities for the victims of violence.

Alison's sufferings might have ended earlier if she had known there was someone for her to turn to, somewhere for her to go. If the gardai had interviewed Alison and her mother away from the father after the first complaint, things might have been different.

It's easy, with the benefit of hindsight, to criticise the inactivity of those who might have helped Alison. But such criticism is pointless unless it's accompanied by positive proposals for change to ensure that no child or young woman ever again has to suffer what Alison suffered.

Kieron Wood
May 1993

PROLOGUE

She sat at the back of the court, twisting her hands nervously. Six feet away, on the bench in front, a small bearded man sat between two prison officers, his head bowed.

The man's patterned seventies shirt, his kipper tie and his rumpled suit made him a pathetic picture. He looked curiously out of place in the bright, new courtroom, like someone who had wandered in by mistake.

In fact, he was the father of the young woman sitting just a few feet away—a woman he had systematically beaten and raped for sixteen of her twenty-seven years.

Michael Cooper had pleaded guilty at an earlier hearing to six charges: that, between 1 January and 28 February 1976, at Loon, Castlecomer, Co Kilkenny, he had raped his daughter Alison Cooper, that he had committed incest with her and that he had assaulted her causing her actual bodily harm. He admitted three similar offences which took place between 1 December and 31 December 1991. The six specimen charges represented fifty-six similar offences.

A door at the side of the court opened and the judge's tipstaff walked in. "All rise in court." Mr Justice Paul Carney walked into the Central Criminal Court and climbed the steps to his seat. He was to pass sentence, but before he did so, the details of the offences were outlined.

Prosecution counsel Joe Matthews, in the traditional wig and black gown, stood up at the front of the court. "This case concerns nightmare events of almost Kafkaesque proportions, a human tragedy on an enormous scale," he began.

"On the night of 16 January 1992, news of an assault on a young woman—an assault of a sexual nature—came to the attention of the police.

"The young woman was in hospital in Kilkenny, suffering from injuries sustained in that violent sexual assault. She was unable to tell police about the events surrounding her condition at that time.

"She lived on a five-acre smallholding in Kilkenny with her father and mother, but when the police heard her story, they were concerned that neither she nor her young son should return to the farm.

"When the young woman had recovered somewhat, she gave a statement to a young woman police officer. That statement indicated that there was a background of ongoing serious offences. The police felt the allegations were so serious that they decided to interview the girl's mother about what she must know.

"On 1 February 1992, Mrs Cooper spoke to police, but she was uncooperative. It was felt necessary to return to the young woman. She was interviewed again on 23 March 1992, at which stage she made a further allegation that her own father was also the father of her child, Ben. The mother corroborated this.

"The matter had now become so horrifying that the police considered it necessary to secure independent medical evidence about her injuries and her admissions to hospitals in Kilkenny.

"The story the young woman had told to doctors when she was taken to hospital was a lie. She was so frightened of her father that she excused her injuries by saying she had fallen on the farm, she had been kicked by an animal, she had fallen downstairs or off her bike."

The courtroom was silent as the barrister began a catalogue of the young woman's injuries. The victim, pathetically dressed in borrowed jeans and a man's jumper, sat anxiously twisting a key between her fingers, occasionally glancing for reassurance at the young policewoman by her side.

"The injuries were horrifying," continued Joe Matthews. "Over a number of years this young woman, as a child, had been admitted to hospital on a number of occasions. She had evidence of nerve injury damage to her fingers, which had been smashed with a lump hammer by her father.

"She had a broken wrist. She had numerous lacerations to the body and scalp which required stitches. She had sustained numerous bruised tissue injuries. She had now permanently lost the sight of one eye due to a kick in the face from a steel-capped boot.

"She had three broken ribs and a broken nose. This was an ongoing tragedy dating back seventeen years. As this young woman grew from a child, she was the subject of unrelenting sexual abuse, rape and incest by her father. Her only sexual experience was with her own father."

Garda Superintendent Vincent Duffe then took the stand. He told the court that the original complaint which had led to the painstaking investigation had come, not from the girl or her mother, but from a third party—possibly the hospital authorities.

The girl had told gardai that, when she was fifteen years old, she had a baby and that her father was the father of that child. As a result, gardai had carried out a six-month investigation, culminating in the arrest of the girl's father.

Next to give evidence was Garda Agnes Reddy, who had befriended Alison Cooper when she was hospitalised. "When I first saw Alison in hospital, she had suffered two cuts which needed stitches. She also had a black eye and numerous fresh bruises on her body, as well as a number of old injuries.

"She seemed very frightened. She found it difficult to express herself about the sexual assaults. From the end of 1976 until the end of 1991, she had been raped and beaten by her father on an almost weekly basis. She was admitted to hospital with her injuries on at least seven different occasions.

"Her father smashed her fingers with a lump hammer, on another occasion her wrist was broken when she tried to defend herself. She is now blind in her right eye after a kick from her father's boot. She has been abused over a period of seventeen years, since she was ten years old.

"When I called at the family home, I found it extremely run down and dark with very dilapidated furniture. On Mr Cooper's chair was a leather strap which Alison said he had used to beat her and her mother.

"Mrs Cooper also made statements to gardai saying that she had been assaulted herself. She always told Alison she would get help tomorrow, but tomorrow never came."

When Garda Reddy had finished her evidence, prosecuting counsel summed up for the judge. "The accused, who is forty-eight years old and un-employed, has a history of ongoing alcohol abuse and addiction over a very long time. The degree of violence in this case is almost unique."

Then Michael Cooper's defence counsel, Barry White, stood to make a plea on behalf of his client. "This is a most unfortunate and tragic situation. The greatest tragedy is that there was not just a cry for help from one individual, but there were several individuals in need of help, care and assistance over a number of years.

"I don't wish to be critical of members of the medical profession, but this is something that appears to have been going on over a large number of years to the knowledge of members of the medical profession and a social worker."

Mr White said his client had spared Alison the humiliation and indignity of reliving her nightmare by pleading guilty, and he asked Mr Justice Paul Carney to be merciful.

The judge leaned forward, his hands clasped on the bench. "The crimes of rape and incest have very different maximum sentences," he said. "The prosecution have accepted that, while rape is in the indictment, I can treat this matter as being one of very violent incest.

"The maximum prison sentence for incest is seven years' penal servitude. I therefore sentence the defendant to the maximum terms of seven years on each of the charges of incest. On the two counts of rape, I also sentence him to seven years' penal servitude and on the two counts of assault, I sentence him to five years. The sentences will run concurrently, making a total of seven years. In view of the fact that he has been in custody for six months awaiting trial, I will suspend the last six months of the sentence."

The judge rose and left the court. Moments later, Michael Cooper stood up, handcuffed to a prison officer, and walked out of the courtroom to begin his six-and-a-half years in jail.

For him, it was the beginning of a sentence. For Alison, it marked the end of a chapter.

1

THE FAMILY

I was born on 28 November 1965 in Bicclescombe Hospital, Ilfracombe, North Devon in England. When we lived in England we had our house and a happy family life. My parents then sold our house in England and bought a house and five acres of land at Loon, Castlecomer, Co Kilkenny.

Mammy and Daddy were both from Devon in the West of England. She was from the seaside village of Lee, near Ilfracombe. Her parents had moved there when they got married. Daddy was from Mortehoe, the next village over. If you cut through from Lee, it was only about six miles away.

Daddy was an only child. Mammy—whose maiden name was Mary Scott—had two sisters, one younger and one older. When they met, Mammy was twenty and Daddy nineteen. At the time, Mammy was working in a draper's shop in

Ilfracombe and Daddy was working in a village called Crackaway. He managed a small farm for a big farmer who lived on another property.

They first met one day in 1963, when Mammy was out walking her dog along the seafront. Daddy came down the road on his motorbike and saw Mammy sitting on the sea wall. He turned round and came back and they began chatting. After that they started going out together.

They went out with each other for nine months before they got married. Their courtship wasn't very eventful; there wasn't much to do in that part of Devon in those days. They'd go for walks together and, once in a while, they'd go on the bus to the pictures in Ilfracombe, five miles away. That was the highlight of the week.

They got married in 1964 and their first child was born six months later. They named her Tanya Alison.

But when the baby was only five weeks old, there was a tragedy. Tanya was in her pram in front of the fire in the farm cottage at Crackaway. Mammy and Daddy were asleep upstairs. Mammy was feeding Tanya every three hours because she was only a small baby when she was born.

There was a spark guard in front of the fire, but somehow a log rolled out onto the mat and it caught fire. Mammy smelt the smoke and woke up. She tried to get downstairs to the baby, but the smoke was too thick, even with all the lights on. Mammy couldn't find Tanya. The fire brigade and the police arrived, but Tanya was dead. Mammy wasn't allowed to see the body before Tanya was buried. Even today, she still won't talk about it. It's just too painful.

They moved out of the farm soon afterwards and went to stay with Granny Cooper in Mortehoe for about nine months. Daddy stopped working on the farm shortly afterwards and went to work on a building site. Then they heard there was a terraced house for sale in Ilfracombe. At the beginning of 1965, they got a mortgage on the two-up, two-down house and moved in. They gutted the inside, put in a new staircase and worked hard together to modernise the house.

Mammy was already pregnant with me when they moved into the house and I was born a few months later. They named me Alison, after my sister who died. Two years afterwards, my sister Tanya arrived. Mammy had a heart attack after Tanya was born and the doctors told her she couldn't have any more children. But Daddy didn't seem too disappointed. He said he'd rather have Mammy living than have another child and risk Mammy dying. She went on the pill and, as far as I know, they had a perfectly normal sexual relationship after that.

I went to school in the Catholic convent in Ilfracombe. Tanya went there for a little while, but then moved to the local primary school. We were happy and we got good reports at school.

Mammy's family wasn't rich or anything but they had enough to get by. Her dad, Bert Scott, was a builder and he was always coming to our house in Ilfracombe. He'd save up enough money to do three or four houses, then he'd sell them and that was it—he'd be off work for three or four months and then start up again. I don't really remember Mammy's mother, Elsie Scott. She died when I was very young.

Grandad died a couple of years ago. I think he knew what was going on between Daddy and me. He came over for a holiday once to Ireland before Ben was born but he'd never come back again. I think he just suspected. He knew Mammy very well; they were very close. He wanted to do something about it but Mammy wouldn't let him. She didn't want him to interfere.

Mammy's two sisters wanted to come to Ireland on holiday but Mammy wouldn't invite them over because of what was going on in the house. When I was in England, visiting Granny Cooper, I didn't really think of telling my aunts what was going on because we weren't really that close to them. We hadn't seen them since we moved over to Ireland. When we saw them in England, we were only there for a week or two for holidays and then we'd come home again.

The last time I saw Mammy's younger sister, Lorna—before Ben was born—I was a bridesmaid at her wedding. Margaret, the elder sister, was married once before. She had two children by the first lad, but they didn't get on, so after a couple of years it broke up. Now she's married again and doing very well for herself.

My happiest memories were in Granny Cooper's house. Rose Mary Cooper—known to everyone as Mary—lives right beside the sea in Mortehoe. On a rough day, the sea spray comes up and hits the window. It was really lovely there at the seaside, especially when my grandad, Frank, was alive. He was a lovely fellow.

The house in England was happy. There were just the four of us: Daddy, Mammy, Tanya and I. Daddy was working as a bus conductor and then he started driving a bread van for Mother's Pride, so he'd go out at half four, five o'clock and we wouldn't see him until nine, ten o'clock at night. Later he went back to working on the building sites. Mother was a cleaner in the local school up the road. In the sum-mer, she'd work as a waitress in a café on the pier.

My father wasn't the sort of man who would show affection. I'd go in and kiss him goodnight, but he would never tuck us into bed or anything. It was the sort of thing any normal child would expect, but we never got that from Daddy. Mother would always come up and say "Are you right?" and she'd turn out the light. But he'd never actually come to see if we were in bed. If we were in bed when he came home, we wouldn't see him until the following night.

When we were young, my father never really hit us. He'd shout at us for not doing something or for telling lies—the sort of thing any child would do to avoid getting into trouble—but he wouldn't usually hit us. He was quick-tempered, but he wasn't really violent. He'd flare up, but then it would all be forgotten.

Off and on there were a lot of women in the house, over a period of time. Even though mother was there, I always wondered if they were Daddy's girlfriends. I never really thought about them then, but as I got older, I kept thinking back to them.

Often at night, I'd come down for a drink of water and I'd see the women there. I used to see four different women there, off and on. One or other of them would be there two or three times a week. Mammy would be out cleaning the school and Daddy would tell me these were just friends who called in for a chat. But the atmosphere wasn't like two friends chatting. I may have been young at the time, but I always sensed something strange in the air, as if I'd interrupted something.

One night there was a woman in the house and her husband arrived. I heard an argument between him and Daddy. When I asked the next day what the argument was about, they said the woman was sick, she had epilepsy or something, and Daddy had been going to give her a lift home.

Mammy's grandmother came from Ireland. Her name was Ellen Lawlor and she was from the

Kilkenny area. Mammy used to say to her she'd like to have a farm one day and her granny would tell her that if she wanted to buy a farm, she should go back to Ireland. Land there was a lot cheaper and easier to buy than it was in Devon. You couldn't buy a few acres in Devon, because if it came up for sale, the big landowners would buy it.

While we were living in Ilfracombe, Daddy was renting a small farm in Mortehoe—a couple of fields really—and he had a couple of cows on it. There was no house or buildings or anything. I can remember walking the cows from one place to another, about four miles away, at five o'clock in the morning. There are so many tourists in Ilfracombe that you wouldn't walk the cows during the day.

In Mortehoe, the National Trust owns all the land. When Daddy was renting from the National Trust, he couldn't build or put up sheds. If you rented a farm, you weren't allowed to develop it. The way it was when you rented it, that's how it had to stay. Daddy was getting fed up with this.

He was always interested in farming, so he took Ellen Lawlor's advice, and went over to Belfast to see if he could find a place. He was unsuccessful, so when he came back to England, Mammy went over to look for a place. She stayed in Wexford, then went up to Carlow and met Tommy Byrne the auctioneer. He told her a property had just come on the market that day at Loon, just outside Castlecomer.

Mammy went to see it and the deal was done there and then. She paid £4,000 for the building on five acres. That was the spring of 1975. My parents sold their house in Ilfracombe and bought the farm outright.

Daddy didn't see the farm until we arrived in Ireland in December of that year. I remember being with Tanya in the back of the van coming over from England. We lay on a mattress watching the lights flashing past as we drove along and I wondered about what my new life in Ireland would be like.

2

ARRIVAL

I was ten years old when we left England to move to Ireland. The year was 1975 and it was Christmas time when we arrived.

The house at Loon was a single-storey, prefabricated house, clad in white aluminium. It was built at the top of one of the fields, next to a mud track. The view was great—you could see out all over the surrounding countryside—but the house was very small.

When you came in the front door, Mammy and Daddy's bedroom was on the left and the bathroom was on the right. We never had a toilet, just a bucket with a plank over it, which Daddy would empty in a pit down the fields every day. We had running water, with electric heating for the hot water. Next to my parents' room was my bedroom, which I shared with Tanya. Across the passageway was the livingroom and off the back of that was the kitchen.

The house should have been built on a concrete raft, but it was just put up on concrete blocks, so it was always damp and cold. Over the years, the water built up under the house and the floorboards rotted. Tanya and I were always getting sick at Loon.

When we caught cold, Mammy would cut up lemons and boil them in a little water and then make us drink the water. She'd also give us a hot mustard bath to let the cold come out through the pores. Two egg-cupfuls of mustard powder in a running bath; it did wonders. When we got wet out on the farm and we couldn't get home straight away, she'd always make us have a hot mustard bath afterwards and often we didn't get a cold at all.

I don't remember Daddy ever being sick, though he was once in hospital in Kilkenny for a week or two to get his gallstones removed. He'd been getting stomach pains for a while, but he wouldn't go and get himself looked at. Then one night it really got bad and he was nearly crying with pain in bed. We phoned the doctor and he sent Daddy into hospital. Mammy drove him in and picked him up when he was discharged. It was the only time we ever had peace in the house. I'd spend all day on the farm and it just seemed so peaceful. He wasn't there to give out to me or correct me. I just felt so free. It was as if I didn't have a care in the world.

Eventually, in 1980, we moved about two miles down the road to a miner's cottage at the Deerpark which Mammy and Daddy bought for £7,000. The house at Loon was boarded up and left. It's still there, with the floors rotted away and the ceilings caving in.

The house at Loon stood on five acres of land. It's not exactly good land—it's very rushy. In a hot summer you could get a good few months out of it, for grazing and hay, but if it comes in wet, you're stuck. Over the years, we had cows or sheep. At one time we had cows and sheep together, calves as well. We would have had two cows, five calves, ten or twenty sheep. We always had chickens and ducks. Mammy loves them. There was always something there that needed your attention.

When we arrived at Loon just before Christmas in 1975, there was no water or electricity—and there was no heating, because it was all electric heating. Neighbours came down to see us and welcome us in and they gave us a loan of an oil heater until we could get sorted out. We had a little camping gas stove for cooking.

It was difficult for Daddy to find a job because he couldn't sign on the dole until he'd been in Ireland a certain length of time. He only got the home assistance, which wasn't much. We didn't get pocket money. If Mammy had any money left at the end of the week, you might get a bag of crisps, but that would be a luxury. Mother was trying to eke out the money until she or Daddy got a job, so we ate pancakes for breakfast, lunch and supper.

Since then, I wouldn't look at a pancake, even on Pancake Day!

For about two years, in about 1979 or 1980, Daddy worked as a night porter and bouncer in the Newpark Hotel in Kilkenny. But he's very quick-tempered and somehow or another he fell out with the owner of the hotel. They were ringing up for him, they wanted him to go back, but he kept the phone off the hook and wouldn't go back. We hadn't had a phone at Loon, but when we bought the house in Deerpark, there was a phone already installed, so Daddy left it in.

He also worked for a coal mining company at Mullaghmore, near Athy, for nearly a year. Then one day they came out and said "That's it," just like that, and closed down the mine overnight. Apart from that, Daddy just worked on the farm and Mammy was the main provider for the family.

The two of them made an odd couple. Daddy's not that tall, but he's very strong. He's always had a moustache and he used to have a beard, but he's shaved that off since he's been in prison. His hair was always long and dirty and he was always untidy looking. If you didn't know him, you'd take him for a travelling person.

There always used to be a smell off him. You know how sometimes you'd go into a room and smell damp or a musty smell. But the smell off Daddy was a real horrible smell. He smoked about seventy cigarettes a day, nearly one after the other, and he didn't wash very often. He'd have a bath once every two months or so and it would nearly make you want to vomit when he came near you. Even though mother always used to have clean clothes ready for him, he'd wear his weekday clothes for two or three weeks without changing them. He hated having clean sheets on his bed—he said they didn't keep you as warm—so mother would only change the sheets on their bed every second week.

Mother was quite different. She's about five foot tall and dark-skinned, with black greasy hair. She always tried to keep herself clean, even if she couldn't have a bath every day. She kept the house tidy, though she wasn't too bothered about cleaning and dusting. But she took a pride in keeping me and Tanya clean and well turned out.

She's a very nice woman to talk to, but she's easily led. If you want her to do something and she doesn't want to do it, she'll resist for a while but eventually she'll do it. She was terrorised by Daddy, so I often felt I couldn't trust her.

When we arrived in Ireland, Tanya and I were a bit worried about starting at the local convent school in Castlecomer because of our accents. We both spoke with an English West Country accent but the other children in the school didn't really make fun of us. At the time there were three other girls in the school from Northern Ireland, so it was a good time to join the school because the accent of the other girls was funny too, so we didn't really get much stick over ours.

Mammy and Daddy told us a lad up the road had horses and that we'd be able to ride them to school. The idea of going to school on horseback was so exciting it made us forget our fears. But when we got there on the first day, it was just like any other school and, when we told the other children we planned to come on horseback, we got taken down a peg or two, as everyone else had come by bicycle, car or bus.

On a typical schoolday, if Mammy was at home— and most days she wasn't, because she was working shifts—she'd come down to our bedroom and call us at about half-past seven. She'd knock on the door: "Come on, are ye awake and ready for school, or what's going on?" She'd try and sound vexed but really she wasn't. Then she'd go back to her room and get dressed. Tanya and I would fight over who should use the bathroom first and who spent longer in there—normal family bickering.

Mammy always washed our clothes by hand— we had no washing machine—and she'd have them clean and ironed, ready for us to go to school.

Mammy wouldn't get breakfast—we never had breakfast in our house. She'd make us tea or coffee and sandwiches for our lunch. We had a choice for the sandwiches—bread and cheese or bread and jam. If she had enough housekeeping money, you might have Branston pickle on your cheese.

We never had sweets or cakes or anything like

that. If Mammy had a few pence left over from the housekeeping, she might give us fivepence to get five penny sweets.

Daddy would be in bed the whole time this was going on. When we left, Mammy would stand on the doorstep and wave goodbye. We caught the school bus about a hundred yards up the road. Everyone used to gather together there, so the bus only had to make one stop.

The bus took about twenty minutes to get into school. The other boys and girls used to talk about what they'd done, where they'd gone with their parents and so on, but Tanya and I didn't really have anything the rest of the kids would be interested in hearing about. We never seemed to do anything exciting—not even going out for drives.

We always had a car or a van. When we came over to Ireland, we had a Moskvich van, but Daddy couldn't get parts for it, so he traded it in for a Hillman Hunter which he bought on HP. But Daddy didn't believe in going out for drives at the weekends. He'd say petrol was too dear and should only be used to go to work or to get the messages. We were just working on the farm most of the time and the other kids at school—girls particularly—didn't want to hear about that. They wanted to talk about the latest pop records, how much money they had, what perfume they'd bought and so on.

At school, we'd go to our own classrooms and the teacher would call the roll. If you had a nun teaching you for the first class, you'd have a few prayers before you started your lesson. We'd break at eleven o'clock for about twenty minutes and we'd try and get in a game of football or basketball. From half-past twelve to half-past one was lunchtime and as soon as we had our sandwiches eaten, we'd play basketball or football again.

School finished at three o'clock—or four o'clock when we got older—and the school bus would be waiting outside to take us home.

If Mammy was at home, she'd have a cup of tea or coffee waiting. I'd change my clothes and then Daddy would be down looking for me to give him a hand around the farm—something like pulling down a tree or holding the wire while he put up a fence. I'd work on until about seven o'clock then go home for my tea. A normal supper would be rashers, sausages and potatoes. The only variation on that—maybe twice a week—would be baked beans or peas. When Mammy wasn't there, I'd do the cooking. I remember Daddy cooking when I was ten or eleven, but then he stopped.

We wouldn't have vegetables every day, but on Sunday we'd have cabbage and turnip, with maybe a pork chop and a bit of gravy. On Saturday, we'd have fish, mashed potato and brussels sprouts. In summer, when the chickens were laying, we'd eat eggs all the time. Every Saturday and Sunday the dinner was always the same.

After supper, I'd do my homework and then,

about half-past nine, I'd go to bed.

The only unpleasant time I can remember at school was when the class was studying the English landlords in history and we sort of felt uncomfortable. We were English and we'd come over from England and, to cap it all, we were Protestants.

Actually, we were members of the Church of England in name only. Religion was never mentioned in our house at all. We wouldn't say any prayers. There was a picture of Our Lady and Jesus in the house, which someone had given Daddy before they died, but it was always covered up with calendars.

The only time we ever went to church as children was when Tanya and I were received into the Church of Ireland a couple of months after arriving in Kilkenny.

My mother told us there would be nobody in the church except the godparents but when we went into the church that Sunday morning, the whole place was packed. I said, "That's it, I'm not going up there." Mammy had to drag me up to the font. The vicar made the Sign of the Cross on our foreheads while we leaned in over the font.

The next time I went to church was when my son Ben was a year old and was baptised into the Church of Ireland. People who went to the Church of Ireland church knew what was going on in our house, but I don't think the vicar knew. Canon Kecgh came to the house to fill in forms when I was getting Ben christened, but he didn't ask me who the father was. I think mother had had a chat with him beforehand and told him the child's father didn't want to be named. Even on the baptismal certificate, where it says "name of father," there's just a line through it.

The Catholic priests never came round to the house because we were Church of Ireland and a Church of Ireland clergyman only came that once.

The only time we ever went to church after Ben's baptism was on Mothers' Day. Ben used to be in the Boys' Brigade and, on Mothers' Day, he'd stand outside the door of the church holding posies of flowers and handing them to the women as they went in. We used to go to church on that day, Mammy and me, just to support Ben.

But now that I've become a Catholic, we go to the Catholic church in 'Comer. I'm changing Ben over as well. He's going to be a Catholic. Well, he's doing the Catholic religion in school and all his friends are Catholic.

I changed over mainly because I'm planning to marry a Catholic, but I also like the Catholic religion a lot better than the Church of Ireland. Sometimes, if our Catholic neighbours were talking about someone who'd died, they'd say "May he rest in peace" or "God bless him," but nothing like that was ever said in our house. I say things like that now, because I'm a Catholic—and I feel better for saying them.

When we were at school, Daddy always wanted us to do well and he made sure I did my homework. He'd give out to us if we weren't concentrating or if we spent too much time playing ball games, but he never really punished me over schoolwork. I wasn't exactly brainy, so I had to put a lot of effort into it, whereas my sister could watch television, not do her homework and the following day, still be able to do well at school. I got two honours and three passes in my Inter Cert before I left school in fifth year.

There were no clubs or anything around, so there was very little to do after school. People used to say I should have been born a boy because I wouldn't do the things the girls did. I would be out playing handball up against the wall with the boys, or I would be playing football.

Daddy wanted me to take up athletics. When he was young, he used to be very good at running. He was on the Devon team, but at that time you had to pay to enter races and his family couldn't afford it, so he gave it up. He was keen for me to do running, but I'm hopeless at athletics.

When I wasn't at school or doing homework, Daddy used to get me to work on the farm. At first, he used to work hard on the farm too, but from 1987 on, he didn't do any of the farm work. He'd just drink and I'd have to do everything myself.

3

THE NIGHTMARE
BEGINS

My grandmother, my father's mother, came to Ireland with us to spend Christmas. A couple of days or maybe a week after Granny left, my father shoved me down on the bed in my bedroom at Loon. He tore off my clothes. He then opened his trousers and pulled down his trousers and underpants and pulled out his penis. His penis was very erect. He kept spreading my legs and pushed his penis into my vagina. It went in the full way because I remember it was very painful and I was bleeding afterwards. My father didn't say anything to me. I thought it was his way of punishing me. That was the first time my father had sexual intercourse with me.

Soon after we arrived in Loon, Granny Cooper came to stay for a month. It was only a couple of days after Granny went home that my father sexually assaulted me for the first time. I was just ten years old. It was the end of January, beginning of February. I can't remember exactly what I had on but I know I had a skirt and some sort of a top. I don't know whether it was a jumper or a shirt. I remember it was fairly cold at the time.

It was the middle of the day, but I wasn't at school. Daddy made me stay at home if he ever needed help on the farm. At the time, Daddy was doing the ditches, fencing them up to get the fields ready to put animals on them. The ditches were fairly bad so they had to be fenced. He was also cutting down trees. If he needed help to pull one down or something like that, I'd have to give him a hand. Mammy wasn't there at the time, because she was out looking for work. She used to go to the dole office and travel around factories, pubs and schools looking for a job.

They say I was close to Daddy. I was his favourite daughter; he always called me his little pet. At this time, he always used to do whatever he could for me. He'd buy me whatever I wanted if he could afford it. He gave me a rocking horse for Christmas when I was nine. But sometimes I felt smothered and needed space to be on my own.

Anyway, on this particular day, I was in my bedroom. I used to go in there just to escape from Daddy. He came into the room and pushed me down on the bed. He didn't say anything to me. He tore off my jumper or shirt and pulled off the skirt. I had a bra on because I was very well developed for a young girl. He just pulled the pants aside and that was it, he was up on top of me. He lay with his whole weight on me. At the time, I didn't know what he was doing, but years afterwards, when I read up about sex, I realised that he had ejaculated into me.

I couldn't understand what I'd done. I just froze, lay there. I didn't know if it was his way of punishing me or if this was natural or what. All I knew was that it hurt a lot. When he'd finished, he just got up and went out of the room. I was just left there, lying on the bed.

I didn't know whether to cry or what to do. I was frightened, but I thought, "If I cry, will he come back down and hit me or give out to me?" I just felt so frightened. Then he shouted to me from the kitchen, "Come on, we've work to do," and we just carried on as normal. So I thought, "Well, whatever I've done, he seems happy enough now." I put jeans and a jumper on and went outside and he carried on: "Bring the rope, bring the saw"—whatever we were doing.

We worked away together until about half-past eight that night. Tanya came home from school and my mother came home and got the dinner and everything went on just like any other happy family. I didn't say anything to my mother because I wasn't sure if it was right or if I'd done something and that was his way of punishing me.

It was only a couple of weeks afterwards that he

came and got me a second time. It would have been February or March 1976. I was still sore after the first time. I remember I didn't go to school that day because I had a stomach bug.

It was in the morning and mother and Tanya were out. He called me into his room. I remember he was in bed and he had socks on. He had his underpants off and I remember he was wearing a vest or T-shirt.

He pulled me down on the bed on top of him. He pulled up my skirt and it seemed to hamper him because it was in the way. He just grabbed my skirt at the waist and tore it and it broke. Then he got on top of me and ejaculated inside me again.

I wasn't having periods at this stage, though I started about six or seven months later. The first two times he raped me, I bled fairly badly. Nobody noticed the blood in my pants because I always washed my bra and underpants—or vest and underpants—myself. I also did my sister's. I used to wash them out in the sink in the kitchen. That was the way we were brought up. We were supposed to do our intimate washing ourselves. Our shirts and jeans and so on could wait until later and mother would do them. Everyone had their own jobs to do.

After this, he used to have sex with me about once every three weeks. I don't remember every incident. After so long, you tend to push them to the back of your mind. But it would seem to be near enough the same every time. He'd push you down on the bed. If you were wearing clothes, he'd tell you to take them off. If you didn't, they'd be torn off you, so in the end you took them off. I mean, having clothes and getting them torn all the time, you were fast running out of clothes.

Mother would say to me, "Jayz, don't come to me this week for money for clothes, I just haven't got it." She didn't actually see the torn clothes because after Daddy tore them he'd take them away and he'd tell her that my clothes had got torn, but I wouldn't have any explaining to do. That's one reason why I always thought Mammy knew exactly what was going on.

One time, I struggled to get up when he was on top of me and he hit me across the face and told me I was a very naughty girl and that's why he was punishing me. He didn't say what I'd done, just that I'd been naughty.

I didn't know what I'd done wrong, all I knew was that Daddy told me I'd done something wrong. So each day, I'd do my chores a different way, I'd change the way I did things to see if that would please him—things like feeding the animals, or getting the dinner, or setting the table. But nothing seemed to matter. He'd still do it to me.

It was after a few months when I was starting to get sore after so much of the same thing that I talked to Mammy. She was taking me into town in the van to get some shopping. She wouldn't see us very often because of the shiftwork and she'd love to catch up on the news. She said to me, "Well, what were you doing all week?" I told her I thought Daddy was after doing something wrong and she asked "Why?" So I told her that he'd pushed himself on me and put his penis into me and ejaculated.

It didn't exactly come out in those words. When we were growing up Daddy used to call his penis his "birdy" and I told Mammy that Daddy had put his birdy inside of me and was moving up and down on top of me. I asked her, "Do all daddies do this or have I done something to make him do it?" She seemed to clam up all of a sudden, though she didn't seem angry or anything. She said, "Don't worry about it, I'll sort this out. It'll be OK. It won't happen again."

That night I heard Mammy and Daddy arguing when we were supposed to be in bed. They were in the kitchen and the television was on, so I couldn't really hear what they were saying, but I could hear the raised voices. My father knew I had told my mother but he didn't say anything.

About two weeks later the same thing happened again.

I was getting very sore at this stage. I was walking queer but nobody at school said anything. They knew I used to ride horses for a neighbour, so they'd assume I was saddlesore, because you'd really be sore after eight or ten hours in the saddle when you weren't used to it. You'd be walking sort of funny.

The way it was at school, the kids would all be

talking about what they'd done at the weekends, what their fathers had bought them, where they'd taken them, for drives and so on. I used to think to myself, "Will I tell them about my father?" but you just wouldn't say anything. You'd make up a story about where your father took you for the weekend and then they'd be happy.

My schoolfriends would say to me, "Can we come down to your house for the weekend?" I'd say, "No, I can't have you coming down." They'd ask why and I'd say, "Ah, it's not safe, the cow would kick you," or something like that and I'd put them off that way. In the end they stopped asking.

I wasn't let go to school every day. Out of the twelve months, I'd be at home at least four or five months on different days. Not long after we arrived at Loon, mother got a job in the textile mills at Castlecomer. When she'd been at that for about six months, she got work in the Braun factory in Carlow. She's been there ever since. She makes parts for hairdryers and razors.

All this time, I was attending the Presentation Convent in Castlecomer. Most of our teachers were nuns. On one occasion, while I was still in the primary school, I was late getting home. One of the nuns kept me behind to talk to me about some lesson I didn't understand. She went out and told the school bus to go on, that I wouldn't be finished for a while. It took me more than an hour to walk the four miles home from school.

I walked up to the house at Loon in my school uniform with my schoolbag on my back. I remember I was wearing a royal blue cardigan, a light blue shirt and real dark blue skirt. I was absolutely worn out after walking all the way home. Daddy just flared up. What was I doing coming home so late from school? Who was I seeing? He thought I was seeing a boy, but I was only about eleven years old and you wouldn't have a boyfriend at that age.

I tried to explain to him what had happened, but he wouldn't listen. He started getting in a real temper, so I just let him shout at me. It was easier than trying to argue with him. Mammy was at work at the time and Tanya was in the house with me. She was about nine years old then and remembers the incident well.

Daddy pulled off my clothes and left me standing in my vest and underpants in the kitchen. He said he'd teach me a lesson for being late. He marched me down to the middle of the field. I was just in my underwear with no shoes or socks on. You could see me from the road and he could see me from the house, so if I moved to get under a ditch or anything like that, he would have seen me.

It was a frosty evening and he made me stand there for four hours. I was blue with the cold. It was only when Mammy came home that she told him to bring me in. She said it wasn't fair, no matter what I'd done, that he shouldn't make me stand outside in the cold. She said he was going to kill me if he left me outside.

I was brought in and Mammy made me go straight to bed. She brought me down soup and hot water bottles. But it took me a very long time to get warmed up.

Tanya told me later that she was watching me out of the window, but there was nothing she could do. She was supposed to be doing her homework in our bedroom but she told me she just stood there and cried. She didn't know why I was being punished.

Although I shared a room with Tanya, I never told her what was going on. I always thought she was too young to understand. Tanya knew about Daddy's bad temper and I think she knew about the physical abuse, but she never knew about the sexual abuse. It normally happened when there was nobody else in the house. Tanya used to play with dolls and read kiddies' books while I was doing the work around the farm. I didn't have all that much time to sit down and read books or watch television. I was physically strong and I suppose I was mentally strong as well, otherwise I'd have cracked up when I was nine or ten.

From the time I was ten until I was fifteen, Daddy would have sex with me about three times a week. If I'd struggle any way at all while he was on top of me, he'd lean up on one hand and hit me across the face and the chest with his clenched fist, so it really hurt.

When Daddy raped me, the smell off him would be repulsive. Afterwards I'd try and have a bath. I'd be there scrubbing at myself with the soap. Even though I didn't have the smell on me, I used to think I smelt of him. I felt so dirty and horrible.

One time the ten-year-old daughter of one of Daddy's friends came round just after Daddy had had sex with me. He said, "Jayzus, she's a nice bird, I'd like to get near her."

He had a quick temper and would lose it easily. One time I got a present from a girl in school, a pen-and-pencil set. It was coming up to Christmas and I asked Daddy for some money to buy her a present back. Tanya wanted some money to give a present to a friend as well. He said, "You're not to ask me for money. You only want it to go out whoring." I was twelve or so at the time and Tanya about ten. We both got beaten for that, for asking for money.

I don't really think he believed that Tanya or I were going out with boys. I think it was just jealousy because I get on well with people and they take me for who I am. He wanted to keep me for himself.

Sometimes he beat me and Tanya with his belt. It was a wide army belt. He'd never have it inside the loops of his trousers. He'd take the belt off and fold it in half with the two ends in his hand and he'd beat you with the doubled belt. He'd beat you across the head, the shoulders, the chest, the legs— literally wherever he could get you. I can't remember him beating Mammy at this time. It was only later, when I was about fifteen, sixteen, that I can remember her getting beaten.

Once, when I was about fifteen, I was beaten and sent to bed for a week. At this stage, we'd moved from Loon to the cottage. It was at the end of a row of cottages, next to a big open field and just across from an old colliery. When you went in the front door of the house, my tiny bedroom—which I shared with Tanya—was on the left. On the right was the small kitchen and leading directly off that was Mammy and Daddy's room.

At the back of the house was a small bathroom. Outside the bathroom, in the hall, was a bookcase where we used to keep our books. I enjoyed reading and had books on gardening and animals and Elvis Presley. Daddy kept his books there too. He used to enjoy books about the Second World War and he'd read a lot of Dennis Wheatley. One of his books which is still there is called *The Satanist*.

Daddy built a lean-to shed on the back of the house and we used to keep fuel there for the kitchen range. We had a big garden out the back of the house and I used to grow plants in the greenhouse. I also used to keep pet birds in cages in the lean-to.

On this particular occasion, I'd been in a car with two other girls and a fella. It was the fella's car and he was teaching one of the girls how to drive in the yard at a neighbour's farm. I reversed the car back into two garage doors and broke them. Your man covered up and said he was driving the car and he'd broken the doors. To avoid a beating, I told Daddy I wasn't in the car at the time, but, about four months later, an old guy who'd seen us went and told my father.

Daddy didn't tell me he'd found out about the lie until after the beating. He just said I was a liar and a cheat and he just kept beating me. He used a whip, something like a horsewhip, made of rounded, thin leather with about five strands on it which would cut you. I was wearing a skirt, underpants and a bra, but he made me take off my T-shirt. He hit me all around the head, the arms, the shoulders, the buttocks and the back. I had welts all over my back and sides.

Mother kept asking him why he was beating me, but he said nothing. He just beat me and told me to get to bed for a week. Afterwards I heard him telling mother it was because I had lied and tried to shift the blame onto the owner of the car.

For three days, Daddy wouldn't let me have any food or any water. After the beating, I had a headache while I was lying down in bed and I was fierce dizzy. I had a lot of bruises and every time I moved or lifted my head, I felt dizzy and couldn't stand. My mother had to help me out to the toilet. While I'd be in the bathroom, I'd take a drink from the bathroom sink as the toilet was flushing. The sound of the flushing covered up the sound of the taps running.

My mother would smuggle me in a sausage or a piece of meat, maybe a slice of bread or a cream cracker—whatever she could put into her pockets without him noticing. She'd stood up to him while he was beating me in the kitchen, but she got a fierce number of welts as well.

4

PREGNANCY

In November 1981 I was in fifth year at school. I noticed I'd missed one period and then in November I started getting pains in my stomach. By Christmas I'd missed three periods and my stomach was getting bigger than it usually was. After Christmas I told my mother I had pains in my stomach and she brought me to [a doctor]. He told me I had too much wind after eating at Christmas, but my mother wasn't happy with that so she took me to get a second opinion. Another doctor told me I was four months pregnant.

When I was fifteen, the year after I did my Inter Cert, I missed two periods. I'd never missed any periods before. I'm hopeless with dates, so I never used to write anything down, when I was supposed to get my periods or anything. Before Christmas I missed a third one, so I told mother I'd missed them. Mammy said, "You couldn't have missed your periods," but I said, "Well I haven't got them. This is the third month now."

Mother said, "We'll take you to the doctor and we'll soon find out." But it went on a further four or five weeks and still she did nothing about it. My stomach was starting to swell up by this time. I was buying bigger and bigger size jeans, but just after Christmas, I couldn't do them up any more. When I'd put on a skirt, you could see the bulge in my stomach.

So just after Christmas, Mammy took me to a doctor. It was the second or third of January. He examined me, but he didn't take a water sample. He put his hands on my abdomen and listened to my stomach and chest and he said, "I can't find anything wrong. I think it's just too much wind after Christmas. You've eaten too much."

He gave me tablets like indigestion tablets and said, "Take these, and if they don't work, come back to me." But Mammy said to me, "That can't be right. You wouldn't stop having your periods just because of wind."

So a couple of weeks later she took me to another doctor. He took a water sample; he had a yoke for testing it there and then. Anyway, he took Mammy outside the door. They were only there a few minutes and she came back in. She looked at me and started crying. I wondered what was going on, why she was crying.

Then the doctor said to me, "You're pregnant.

You're four months pregnant, and your baby is due in May." There I was, sitting there, going to have a baby, and me hardly more than a baby myself.

I didn't know anything about children at this time, how you got them or anything like that. I'd never spoken about it with the girls at the convent because the nuns would hear you and sex was a taboo subject. We didn't do biology and my class didn't take chemistry. We did subjects like history, geography, home economics and that sort of thing. But even in home economics it was, "The man and wife married and after a couple of years they had children," but you weren't exactly told how they had children.

I knew how the animals on the farm did it, but I didn't relate that to people. The AI man used to come round and artificially inseminate the cows, so I didn't often see animals mating. I thought you had to stay in bed overnight—or at least a couple of hours—to get pregnant. It didn't occur to me that by just getting into bed and having it done to you and then getting up again, you'd get pregnant. I didn't know exactly what happened, that a man had to put his penis into the woman's vagina. I thought it just somehow happened when you were in bed. I suppose I was very stupid when I was younger.

Well, after the doctor told me I was pregnant, Mammy pulled herself together and stopped crying. Coming home together in the car, she said to me,

"Is Daddy the father of your baby?" I said, "Yes," and she said to me, "I'll put a stop to this." That was only the second time I'd spoken to her about Daddy abusing me. The first time, I'd taken Mammy at her word that she'd get it stopped or do something about it. When she didn't do anything about it, I thought there was nothing that could be done.

When I got home, Mammy told Daddy I'd been to see the doctor and that I was pregnant. He just said to me, "Well, after all that poking and prodding, you'd better go and lie down. Go and rest yourself. We'll do the jobs ourselves tonight."

When I was in my bedroom, I could hear them arguing in the kitchen. I can plainly remember hearing Mammy say, "You shouldn't have done it. Why did you do it?" What his answer was, I don't know, I couldn't hear. But Mammy was really, really vexed over it. The next thing I heard china getting broken in the kitchen, plates and cups. But when I went into the kitchen, when they called me for tea, it had all been cleared up.

Daddy denied that he was the father of the baby. He told people that I was a whore, that I'd go with anything in trousers. I used to have men ringing me up at three o'clock in the morning when the pubs chucked out. "How much do you charge? What positions do you do?" I just used to listen silently without answering, wishing desperately that I was somewhere else.

At that time, Granny Cooper used to come over

and stay three or four months at a time. She was there when I was pregnant and at the time Daddy let me go to a disco on a couple of occasions. He had to keep up appearances in case Granny wondered how I'd got pregnant. She'd ask, "Who's Alison going out with? I haven't seen her with a regular boyfriend." Daddy used to tell her I'd go with anyone, that I was a real whore and so on.

But some of my very good friends realised that I wasn't going out with anyone, so how could I be pregnant? They saw me coming up to their houses covered in bruises and so on, and they knew what had happened and they were horrified, but they never really said anything to me and they never did anything about it.

I went to school up until about February 1982, when I was six months pregnant. I was fairly big and I think the teachers knew, but they didn't say anything. Nobody knew who the father was, but, after I had left school, the boys who had been friendly with me would say, "Sure, it doesn't matter who the father is. You're not the first and you won't be the last to get pregnant. It's not the worst thing in the world. Just get on with your life. You're still only a girl and you have to have your education." The lads were OK, they didn't ask who was the father or why I got pregnant or say I shouldn't have done it. But the girls ganged up on me. They used to say I had so many boyfriends, I didn't know who the father was. But that wasn't true. I didn't have any boyfriends when I was going to school because I was too afraid.

I didn't tell anyone who the baby's father was. I told my best friend a couple of days before I left school that I was pregnant, but she didn't ask me who the father was. She just asked if I was going to keep the baby or give it up for adoption. Even at that stage, I wanted to keep the baby. I couldn't think of giving it up. I'd seen the animals having babies and I knew there was pain involved, but I thought that, in the end, it would be worth it.

Even while I was pregnant, Daddy continued to have sex with me. One time, he said to me if the baby was a girl, my bags would be packed before I had time to come out of the hospital. But if it was a boy, I'd be allowed to stay in the house. He always wanted a boy and Mammy couldn't give him one.

Not long after the pregnancy was confirmed, Daddy beat me very badly. I was up at the farm at Loon. We kept three pet lambs up there at the time. I was supposed to feed them, but they didn't seem hungry. It was about twelve o'clock at this time and I'd been up at the farm since half-past six in the morning. I was starving so I said to myself that if I walked home to the Deerpark, got myself a bit of dinner and walked back up, I could stay at the farm for the rest of the afternoon. I'd be able to feed the lambs, finish up the jobs and go home about six o'clock.

Daddy had gone up to a neighbour's house. He

was supposed to drive your man into town and do some work there and get home about half-past seven that night. I said to myself, "He won't know the difference, give or take an hour, when the lambs were fed," so I walked home. There were two potatoes in the house, so I peeled them and made them into chips and had them with an egg.

I had just started eating it when he walked in the door. He gave out something fierce to me. He said that I should have fed the animals first, before I fed myself. Wasn't I always brought up to know that the animals come first?

I started shouting at him that I was hungry too, that I was pregnant and had a baby to feed. I needed something to eat. I said the lambs hadn't been hungry and that they could wait until I went up to the farm. I only had about two chips gone off the plate and what did he do but throw the whole lot into the fire.

He took the belt off his trousers and started hitting me around the face and stomach. He was really ranting and shouting that the animals came first, people didn't count.

When he'd finished beating me, I had to walk up to Loon and do the jobs. I stayed there until half-past six that night before I was allowed to come home and get something to eat.

Apart from that time, Daddy didn't hit me too much when I was pregnant. I wasn't working too much with the animals because Daddy was afraid a cow would kick me or something, so Tanya was doing my jobs. But she's not very good with animals because she's afraid of them and they know that and it makes them nervous. So Daddy was giving her fierce beatings, and often I'd step in and take the beatings instead of her.

At times during the pregnancy, I really wanted just to lose the child. But I didn't make a great effort to get rid of it. A couple of times I drank a cup of washing-up liquid, but it just made me sick. My periods never came back and I didn't start haemorrhaging or anything. I wanted to lose the child, but I didn't want to hurt it. I didn't want to do anything which would leave it living and handicapped. When the washing-up liquid didn't work, I didn't try anything else.

The day before Ben was born, I was still in bed at around midday. I'd been allowed to have a lie-in. I'd been getting fierce pains in my stomach but I thought it was just cramps.

Tanya was in the kitchen when my waters broke. I called her in and said, "I'm after wetting the bed." She said, "Don't be so stupid" and went and got Mammy, who was getting ready to go to work. Mother had a look and said, "That's it, you're going into hospital. Your time is up."

5

BIRTH

Ben was born on 20 May 1982. I was fifteen when he was conceived and sixteen the November before he was born. Ben, my son, is definitely my father's child. I did not have intercourse with anyone else. My mother filled in all the forms and registered Ben's birth. I was kept in hospital for seven days after the birth and then returned home to Deerpark.

Mammy took me into St Luke's Hospital in Kilkenny and signed me in and I was left there in the corridor, waiting for a nurse or a doctor to come and see me. I didn't blame Mammy; she had to get to work. But I thought that perhaps Daddy might have come in with me to see that I was OK.

Eventually, after about an hour, I was put into the labour ward. This was Wednesday afternoon at about three o'clock. I didn't have Ben until half-past nine on Thursday night. It was really, really painful. Nobody came to see me. There were no friends or members of the family there when the baby was born.

The nurses were very good and kind and tried to make things as easy as they could for me. They'd say, "Don't worry, when you see the baby, you'll fall in love with him." But it was just so horrible being left on my own. I had nobody to tell me what was going to happen, though the nurses did a good job of trying to explain. I remember one nurse telling me, "Now hold your legs up here with your hand." Here I was, looking down the table, and my legs floating off away in the distance.

I think there was a doctor and two nurses there when Ben was born. I wouldn't take anything for the pain because I wanted the birth to be natural. I remember the nurse saying to me, "Push a bit harder."

"I can't."

"Well you're going to have to," she said, "because his head is there but he's not coming." All I remember is the pain.

Ben weighed eleven pounds when he was born and his shoulders were so broad that when he came out he tore me. I had to have eight stitches. They took him away and washed him, then brought him back and put him into my arms. He had a lovely head of black hair and I just couldn't part with him. A social worker came to see me that day and asked whether I wanted to get the baby adopted.

After all, I was only sixteen, and I couldn't rear him. But when I looked at him that day, just wrapped in blankets, I couldn't part with him. I took a photo of him the day he came out of hospital. He was huge and he was gorgeous.

My mother agreed. She'd come in to register the birth. She didn't put any name down for the father. She said, "No, don't give him up, he's beautiful."

I learned about sex only when I was in hospital having Ben. There were magazines there with letters all about sex and people having problems with their sex life. I was reading a magazine one day and I just asked a couple of the nurses about it and they said to me, "Don't you know what sex is all about?" I said no and one said to me, "Well, you're after having a baby. You should know." Then another nurse came over to me. She was the kind of nurse you could talk to. She said, "Do you not understand it?" and I said no, so she explained it to me. It was only then that I realised what had been happening.

After the birth I was put in a room with three other girls. One of them was very snooty and wouldn't talk to me, but the others would chat. I've kept in contact with them ever since. One of the girls was an unmarried mother as well and she'd say to me, "My boyfriend's coming in tomorrow. Is yours coming in?" I just made up a story that my boyfriend had gone to England, that he was working and he'd be back soon. At this time, I began to realise that what Daddy was doing was wrong. I was just so ashamed that I didn't know what to say to people.

Daddy doesn't like hospitals and he only came in once to see me. Ben was lying beside my bed in a cot. Daddy took one look at him and said, "Jayz, he looks just like a little monkey. Throw him out the window and see will he bounce." And that was it. Within a few minutes, he left.

But I heard from neighbours that he was really proud when Ben was born. He went out drinking while I was in the hospital and told a couple of his friends in the pub, "I'm a grandfather. I'm delighted. She gave me a grandson."

He acted like a grandfather. He'd lean in over the pram or cot and talk to Ben all right, but, for the first eighteen months, he'd never play with him. One time at home, when Ben was about a year and a half old, the phone rang when I had the baby in my arms. Daddy would never answer the phone. I put the baby down on Daddy's knee while I answered the phone. Before that, Daddy would never hold on to Ben or play with him, but after that, he did.

After the baby was born, we had social workers coming in to see us in the hospital, but they weren't able to be of any assistance to me.

They said my mother had filled in all the forms for a lone parent's allowance—it was the unmarried mother's allowance at the time. They said, "You'll get that and you'll get the child allowance and we

can fix you up with a few blankets for the child."
They did let me have some blankets, but that was
all.

I met social workers again on several occasions.
Daddy wanted adoption papers drawn up for him
and Mammy to adopt Ben. A social worker drew up
the papers but I never signed them. Later, when
Daddy was in prison, he wrote a letter to Mammy
saying, "Inquire with the social worker about the
adoption papers." He thought the papers had been
drawn up and signed and sealed, because when I
left hospital in January 1992, he went to the gardai
and told them I'd kidnapped his son.

I had Ben on the Thursday and stayed in the
hospital for a week. Mother came to pick me up.
When I got home, they had everything ready for
the new baby. Then, three days after I arrived home,
Daddy had sexual intercourse with me again.

6

HOMECOMING

After I came home from hospital after Ben being born, my father came into my bedroom and pushed me down on the bed. He started saying, "I want a bit of sex." This time I really knew it was wrong and I said to him, "Don't do it, this is wrong." He hit me around the face and breasts. He pushed me down on the bed and I just lay there with his hands beside my sides and let him have sexual intercourse with me.

After Ben came home from the hospital, he wasn't settling very well. I used to have a bath and go to bed and get a bit of sleep while Ben was sleeping.

The Sunday after I arrived home, I was just coming out of the bathroom and getting ready to go to bed for an hour. It was the middle of the afternoon. I just had a dressing gown on. I don't know where Mammy and Tanya were.

This time, Daddy just said to me, "I want a bit

of sex." At this stage I'd read up on the facts of life
and all about sexual intercourse and I knew what
was happening. I said, "You can't do this, it's wrong.
You'll be put in jail for this." He said, "You won't
tell anyone. If you tell anyone, I'll be put away for
life. Anyway, you like it."

Rather than have the dressing gown torn off me,
I took it off. But I was wriggling to try and prevent
him putting his penis into me. I was very sore
because I'd had dissolving stitches put in after the
birth and they were still in. Since I couldn't tell
anyone, I thought if I just started protecting myself
by putting up a fight and not letting him enter me,
he'd give in and he wouldn't do it. But it didn't
work. While I was down lying on my back, he was
just stronger than me and I couldn't resist. He just
punched me across the face and chest and hit me
in the stomach and then he started hitting me with
a belt.

He was smoking at the time and he put his hand
across my neck and held me down and burned me
all over the chest with his cigarette. He'd leave it
until you could smell the skin burning. I couldn't
scream out because I would have woken the baby.
I was just there, silently crying to myself. The tears
were running down my face and I just couldn't
stop crying. The pain of it was awful. I still have the
marks under my breasts from the cigarette burns.

Not long after this, while I was still sore from the
birth, he was trying to get up on top of me and I

lifted my leg and gave him a knee into the groin. It really hurt him, but in the end I got the worst of it. He hit me across the face with his belt and punched me again and again. I felt really dizzy afterwards. I had to sit down for about an hour. Every time I lifted my head, I felt dizzy.

About this time, when Tanya was thirteen or fourteen, she was seeing a fella called Tom—the guy she's married to now—and Daddy didn't like him.

At that time, Daddy wouldn't let us go to discos, but about once every three weeks, we'd be allowed to go to the school disco. It would start at seven o'clock and be over at eleven. Tom liked to go for a drink first, so he wouldn't turn up until late and he'd often be drunk.

Once when Tanya and I went to the school disco, Daddy drove us in and asked us what time we wanted to be picked up. We said not to bother because there was a bus going home. Tanya wanted to meet Tom, so she left the disco at about half-past ten.

She arranged with me to meet me down the road from the house at half-past eleven, but said not to go into the house until we were both there. I was there at about a quarter past eleven and waited and waited. It got to half-past eleven and there was no sign of her. A quarter to twelve, still no sign.

At twelve o'clock I decided that if I stayed out any longer, I'd really be in trouble. I was starting to walk over towards the house when I saw the outside light come on. Daddy came out in a fury. He told me I'd been with some fella. He was shouting and roaring. Who was I with? The disco was over since eleven o'clock and where had I been?

It turned out that Tanya had got a lift home and had gone straight in. She told Daddy she'd been with a couple of girls and that I'd been talking to some other girls and she didn't know where I'd gone.

He told me he'd gone to 'Comer looking for me and the nuns at the disco had told him I'd gone home with this fella, but I knew that wasn't true.

He said Tanya could go out and come home on time and I couldn't. That night I really got beaten badly. He broke my nose. He said I was never going to a disco again.

Some time afterwards two gardai came out to the house and sat Tanya out in their car and told her, "Finish your education. If you still want to see Tom, carry on after that." But she wouldn't listen. She said no, she loved him and was going to be with him.

Soon after that, Tanya was on the floor in the kitchen in the Deerpark doing her homework. I was getting the dinner and I asked her to peel a turnip. Daddy was in bed. We thought he was asleep.

I said to Tanya, "Peel a turnip there for me, will you, while I do the spuds," but she said, "Look, I've this to do. Hold on and I'll do it in a minute." Then she got up and turned on the television and sat down and started reading a book. I said, "Go on, peel a turnip for me, I'm in a hurry."

She gave me some saucy answer. What it was, I can't remember, but Daddy came bursting out of his room next to the kitchen and he smashed her over the head with the turnip. Then he hit her over the head with one of those push-along carpet sweepers. She had to have three stitches.

After I put Ben down that night about six o'clock, Tanya said to me, "I've had enough. I'm going."

"Don't bring me into it," I said. "I don't mind as long as you know what you're doing and you're happy."

"Don't worry," she said, "there'll always be a place for you in our house."

About two o'clock the following morning she climbed across my bed which was under the window and she squeezed out of the tiny opening at the top of the window. I passed out her clothes to her and she went. She never came home again.

She lived with Tom at his family's house in Clogh. They had their first baby when she was nineteen and, three years later, she changed her religion and she got married to him. They've got three children now, two girls and a boy.

I see Tanya now and then, but we were never allowed to talk to her when Daddy was at home. One time, after she'd had her first baby but before she got married, she phoned up home after a row with Tom. Daddy said, "If you're at the phone box in five minutes, I'll bring you home." But when he went up she wasn't there, so when she phoned up again looking to talk to us, he wouldn't let her. He told her, "You've made your own choice now. You stay there."

When she got married, she wanted to invite Mammy and me to the wedding, but she couldn't because she knew Daddy wouldn't let us go, or if he did let us go, he'd go too and ruin it for her. So they got married all by themselves.

Four or five months after Ben was born, we were having dinner in the kitchen. Tanya had left home by this time and Daddy was having sex with me every couple of weeks.

Daddy said to me, "You're old enough now, you'd better go on the pill." Mammy asked why and he said, "Well she might find a boyfriend and she might need to go on it."

They discussed the arrangements and Mammy took me in to a doctor. He asked why I wanted to go on the pill. Mammy said, "Well, she has one child and she doesn't want to get pregnant again." He asked what age I was and Mammy said, "Sixteen." So he just wrote out a prescription for the pill. But Mammy never asked me whether Daddy was still doing anything to me.

I hated what was being done but I went on the pill because I just couldn't go through having another child. I'd told the social workers and they wouldn't do anything. I'd told Mammy and *she'd* done nothing. I thought, "Well, I'm just going to have to live with it." I was better off being on the pill than having another child.

7

LIFE AT HOME

Ben stayed in the pram until he was nearly two years old. At this stage Tanya had left home so I took Ben into a cot in my bedroom. He stayed in the cot until he was five, then he went into my parents' bedroom in a single bed. My father insisted that Ben's bed went into their bedroom.

In a house where I had no happiness, just sheer terror most of the time, Ben was a ray of sunshine. When you'd put him up on your knee and give him a little present, his whole face would light up. It was really wonderful and you felt happy because of his happiness.

Over the years, Ben asked several times who his father was. I told him that when he was fifteen or sixteen—when he was old enough to understand— I'd tell him everything. He just assumed his father was someone who didn't love me and went away.

But he was hurt when he found out who his father really was. The day of the court case in March 1993, I got home at ten to six and it had been on the half five news. He was listening to it with Mammy and he heard it. He said he never wanted anything to do with Daddy again. He doesn't ever want to see him or hear from him.

When Daddy was first in prison, he made a wooden plaque with a photo of Ben in it and sent it to him. But Ben just wanted to burn it. I wouldn't let him. The plaque is nicely done and maybe Ben will want it later on when the anger and the hurt go away.

Several people have said to me that, because of the way Ben was conceived, there might be something wrong with him. But I keep a check on him, on his homework and schoolwork. His eyes and ears are checked regularly and he seems fine. He's not mentally handicapped or anything like that. In fact, he does very well at school. The teachers say they have to slow him down, as he sometimes gets too far ahead of himself. He loves reading and he's very good with animals.

He hasn't seen a psychologist, because we're leaving him as he is for the time being. When he gets older, if his attitude starts to change, then he'll get treatment. I've had a nurse out from Kilkenny looking through his schoolbooks and she said he was fine, to leave him as he was. He gets on well with his own age-group, but he's also really gentle with younger kids and enjoys looking after them.

Ben's always called me Alison and he calls my parents Mammy and Daddy. He loves Mammy and thinks she shouldn't have been hurt. He saw a lot of the violence because he was there nearly all the time it was going on. He saw me being stripped, he saw Mammy and me being beaten. When he was nine, he saw Daddy pull off my shirt and bra.

He was close to Daddy up until about 1991. Every Christmas there used to be a party in Ben's school and I'd bake something like apple tart or sausage rolls and take them up to the school. While we were setting up the tables for the parties, the children would be up in the church for the Christmas service, then they'd come back to the school for the party.

This particular time, I couldn't go to the party because I was killing the turkeys at the farm. Daddy was at home drinking poitin. Ben had been given a toy at the party, a little tractor. In fact, I'd bought it, but the children thought Santy had given them the presents.

When Ben arrived home from the party, he came in and looked at me, then he looked at Daddy and put the tractor back in the bag and put it out in the car. He knew Daddy was drunk and he just didn't want his toy broken, because that's what would have happened.

Later that night we were up at the farm killing turkeys. Daddy took some of the turkeys in the back of the van, but he was so drunk he crashed into a wall further up the lane. He came back to the farm and started hitting me and Ben around. Well, he didn't really hit Ben so much as push him out of the way. But the child was so hurt afterwards. He said, "Why doesn't Daddy like me?"

Apart from Ben, the other love of my life at this time was the farm at Loon. After Ben was born and I'd left school, I'd spend five days a week up at the farm at Loon. Those are among my happiest memories.

Daddy would drive me up to the farm and I'd arrive there about eight o'clock in the morning. We'd bring up tubs of water and a bin of food for the animals. Daddy would be sat in the shed drinking and I'd do the work. The animals seemed nervous when he was around. Whether it was because of his drinking or because of his voice when he was shouting and giving out, I don't know. It was almost as if they didn't want him there. Everything went better when I was there on my own. The animals were quieter and more easy-going.

Loon was my little safe place. Sometimes a neighbour would come down to ask Daddy's advice about horses and cattle and so on. You couldn't be sure when he'd come down, but he'd just stay talking to Daddy and that kept the two of them out of my way. I didn't particularly like this neighbour, but he was still a welcome sight coming down across the fields.

Floss, my dog, would greet me when I arrived.

She's a collie cross. She's very good with the animals and wouldn't hurt them. She'd round up the sheep for me, but she wouldn't chase the chickens or worry the cows.

The first thing I'd do would be to open the little hatch in the shed to let out the eleven Aylesbury White ducks and a drake, so they could go down to the stream nearby.

We kept four calves in the shed—Curly, Larry, Mo and Bluey. When I'd go in to collect the ducks' eggs, the calves would get up and start licking my trousers. It was a great feeling to be wanted. In the house, I only saw myself as an object to be abused, but at Loon when I was on my own, the animals showed me affection and it was great to feel I was needed. I'd go through into the ducks' pen, pick up their eggs and put them in an old metal can. I'd wash out their feed dishes and the water dish in the stream and put fresh food and water in the shed for them.

The ducks are bedded up with hay and straw, so they're fairly clean and dry, but they'd have to be cleaned out every three weeks. Then I'd put out food in the shed for the cows. They'd eat bread, potato peelings, carrot peel—the only thing you wouldn't give them would be onion peels, they wouldn't eat them—but carrot, parsnip, turnip, potato, cabbage, brussels sprouts, anything like that they'd eat.

We always had two cows at Loon. Our first cow

was Pokey, a Poll Angus, and we had her for about ten years. When Ben was about two years old, he'd come in from the field holding on to Pokey's tail. He'd give her a kick in the leg and say "Geddup Pokey" and she'd wander in with him swinging on her tail. She'd never kick him.

When I'd arrive, the two cows would be out in the field—a friesian called Lulu and a whitehead called Whiteface. Lulu was born at Loon and Whiteface was bought in later. As soon as they heard the car arriving, they'd start to come in. When I'd leave the shed, the two cows would be waiting at the gate.

I'd open the gate, call the cows and walk back into the shed. I'd leave the door open and just stand back. The two cows are so used to coming in that they'd each go to their own trough. There are two chains hanging up on nails. I'd put a chain round the neck of each of them and that was them tied.

I'd get a bit of water in a bucket with a splash of washing-up liquid and wash off the cows' udders before the calves sucked. Then I'd let the calves out of their pen. When they're newborn and you're trying to get them to suck, it's a hassle making sure that the same two calves always go to the right cow, but eventually they get the hang of which cow they're to go to and which side they're to go to. It's just natural.

The calves would suck for maybe twenty minutes,

half an hour, depending on how much milk the cows had when they came in. I'd stand there watching them. Thomas, the ginger cat, would hang around the calves' heels, licking up any bits of milk they spilled. Sometimes the cow would kick and you'd have to give out to her. Other times the calves could get very rough and puck with their heads to get the milk down. You'd have to give the calf a tap then to stop it, otherwise it could damage the cow's udder. The udder is like a woman's breast. If you give a woman a punch in the breast, it leaves a big bruise or a lump.

When the calves had finished sucking, I'd put them back in their stall and wash off their saliva from the cows' udders. Then I'd sit in under each cow on an upturned bucket and strip her out—that is getting each quarter of the udder and teasing the remnants of the milk out to stop her getting mastitis. If there was enough milk, I'd put it into bottles and keep it in cold water during the day and we'd use it for the house. If there wasn't enough, I'd give it to the cat.

I always had to do Lulu first, then Whiteface, otherwise Lulu would sulk and not drink her water. Then I'd give the cows as much water as they wanted and let them back out into the field—Lulu first, then Whiteface.

After the cows had left the shed, I'd clean out their stalls—sweep up the muck, shovel it into a wheelbarrow and put it on the dungheap. Then I'd wash out the place with disinfectant. While the stalls were drying, I'd see to the chickens.

I'd give them layer's pellets and barley, pick up their eggs and let out the thirty-three Rhode Island Red hens and the rooster. We'd get between twenty and thirty eggs a day during the laying season. Mostly we ate them ourselves. We had friends and neighbours that would take them too, but there weren't that many left after you'd made omelettes and used them in sponges and apple tarts and stuff. Everyone in our house was fond of scrambled eggs, so you'd use a couple of dozen for that every week.

With the sheep, the work was easy. We used to have about twenty of them out in the paddock. We'd buy them in as old hoggets, coming up to second-year ewes, and if they were any good at lambing we'd keep them for two or three years. We'd borrow a ram from a neighbour for mating.

Some of the sheep could be in lamb when we'd buy them in. Daddy taught me how to put my hand in under their stomach next to the udder and really lift up. If the lambs are there you feel them on your wrist. I know father abused me a lot of the time, but I'm grateful for what he taught me about animals.

The sheep would be out in the field all winter long. I'd just give them a bucket of barley and tub of water, and every second day I'd fill up the hayrack. If there were lambs there, I'd take down some ewe and lamb mixture.

There were only two sheep I had names on. One had sheeprot very badly and we had to cut off the toe part of her front and back foot to save her. I used to call her Granny because she used to hobble around. The other one I knew was Blackie, a little black-faced mountain lamb. She'd eat toast—not bread, only toast.

Some people say sheep are really timid animals, but I have no problem with them. I can look into a sheep's eye and tell you if she's sick or well, exactly what medicine she needs, when she needs it and how much she needs.

By about half-past eleven, all the jobs would be finished and I'd sit down with a cup of tea, before feeding the dog and the cat. Then, for the rest of the day, there'd be nothing really to be done but sit around in the sunshine. I'd find a nice little sunny spot under the hedge and sit there, listening to the birds or watching the animals eating, the chickens picking in the grass, the ducks bathing, the lambs racing around the field. It would be lovely just to sit and watch them.

I used to take books up there—mostly history books or books about animals I'd borrowed from friends. It was the only chance I had to learn about the latest discoveries about animal welfare. Daddy didn't believe in buying newspapers and he wouldn't allow anyone to buy any magazines or farming journals.

About five o'clock, I'd call the hens, and most of

them would go into the shed by themselves. I'd round up the few that were still scratching outside and drive them into the shed. Then I'd bring in the cows and milk them again, put them back out in the field and wash out the standings, get the ducks in and, by that time, it would be nearly six o'clock and I'd be ready to go home.

It's a great life. In the deep of the winter particularly, when there's snow on the ground or it's real frosty and the animals are munching away and contented, then you know you did your best for them. Ben and the animals were all that made my life worth living.

8

THE BEATINGS

In May 1985, a few days after Ben's third birthday,
my father took the bar off the front of the cooker by
yanking it off. He was drinking at the time. I put my
hand up to defend myself and he hit me across the
wrist. I went to bed with my hand paining me. When
I got up the next morning I was holding it across my
stomach and he told Mammy to take me to the doctor.
I went to St Luke's Hospital and I told them in casualty
I had fallen when playing football.

Daddy was really violent, though he wouldn't
generally be violent with people outside the family.
He would pick up cups, plates, a saucepan—
anything, as long as he could hurt you with it.
When he was drunk he'd pick arguments with
people in pubs and then walk out. He'd arm-wrestle
with them and then say that he'd won and they
hadn't.

The only time he ever actually hurt someone outside the family was one time when he was drunk. He was getting into the car to bring Mammy home and this man came up and said, "Why don't you go and see your grandchild?" I don't know exactly what was said, but Daddy beat the man up in the car park.

Daddy used to wear a pair of knee-length cowboy boots, brown with steel toe-caps. He always wore them when he was going out anywhere. He had those boots on and when the man was on the ground, unconscious, didn't Daddy stamp on his head. He kept grinding the boot flat into his face. This happened on a Thursday evening at about half-past four. Your man didn't come round until Saturday night at ten to twelve. The doctors were really getting worried. They were saying he wasn't going to come round; they were worried he'd die.

The only person who ever stood up to Daddy for beating me up was a lad called Alan Nash from Clogh. He was known to his friends as Bamba.

Bamba was nineteen and very well-built because he lifted weights. He was known as the peaceful giant. We'd gone to school together. Whenever Daddy and I went into the pub in Clogh, Bamba would be there playing pool. Instead of coming over and talking to me, he'd just say hello to me in passing, then he'd always sit down and talk to Daddy, who had great time for him.

On two occasions when Granny was over for

Christmas, when I was about twenty-one or twenty-two, Bamba came down to the house and asked Daddy if he could take me out for the night. It wasn't like boyfriend and girlfriend. It was more of an excuse for getting me out of the house. We'd get the bus at half-past ten from Clogh and go to Pedigree Corner, a big disco place in Ballylynan. The bus would then drop us back at two or three o'clock.

Daddy would give me a lift up to the pub in Clogh. He'd go in to make sure Bamba was there, then he'd leave me and he'd be waiting before the bus got back.

Bamba knew Daddy beat me up but he didn't know about the sexual abuse. One day, Daddy was in the pub and I asked him to come home and he started hitting me. He just slapped me across the face. Bamba turned round to him and said, "Why did you do that? The girl's fed up and she wants to go home."

Daddy said, "I'm not ready to go home yet."

"Well," said Bamba, "you may not be ready, but she's fed up. Why don't you think about her?"

Daddy was so surprised that he left the pub. We went home and Daddy just went to bed. I think he was shocked that a younger chap had actually stood up to him.

Last year Bamba went out to a pub in Kilkenny. There were two guys rowing. He went over to them and said, "Look lads, you've had enough. Now why don't you go home and sort out your differences tomorrow?"

As he turned round to walk off, he was stabbed. They couldn't stop the bleeding and he died while they were operating on him.

Unfortunately for me, there was nobody like Bamba around most of the times Daddy started beating me up. One time, in May 1985, Daddy was ranting and raving in the kitchen for a long time. He grabbed the bar across the front of the range. The screws were loose and the bar came off. He was going to hit me across the face with it and I put up my hand to defend myself. He brought it down on my hand and broke my wrist.

On another occasion, in 1981 or 1982, he pulled the bar off the cooker and hit my mother straight across the forehead with it. Her head was split open. She just collapsed onto the couch and she lay there for four hours, out cold. He didn't say, "Oh God, I've killed her," or "Is she hurt bad?" He just took one look at her crumpled on the sofa and went to bed.

It took me a long time to stop Mammy's head bleeding. I used cold cloths and took packets of frozen food out of the freezer to try and get the swelling down. The following day Daddy wouldn't let her go and get it stitched. Every time she moved, it would start bleeding again. She has two white scars there now.

One night Daddy had hit me over the head with

a saucepan—actually we still have that saucepan with a dent in the middle of it—and then he hit Mammy over the back of the head with it. I just got a lump, but she was cut. It was a friend of hers at work who noticed her bleeding in the factory. They called the doctor and he came up and stitched her but nobody asked how it had happened.

Another time, he hit me with a bar across the ribs and my skin burst. It was a small gash, but deep. I should have had six stitches, but he wouldn't let me go to the hospital until the gash had healed up. I couldn't bend down or run or anything. Eventually, when I went to St Dympna's Hospital in Carlow, they said my ribs were cracked. They said they might have been broken originally, but they'd started to heal. Afterwards when we were looking for the X-rays for the court case, we found they'd lost them.

I was X-rayed in St Dympna's on another occasion at the end of 1987 or the beginning of 1988. Daddy had kicked me on the back of the legs and knocked me down. When I was down he kicked my ribs.

I've had my nose broken several times. That's why it's so crooked. Sometimes, if you had a row and something got broken and fell on the floor, he'd tell you to pick it up. You'd be down with a dustpan and brush sweeping it up but you'd always watch your back because he'd come up behind you and kick you between the legs to try and hurt your private parts. That was one of his favourite tricks.

He'd kick you from the front or the back. You'd be watching your back and he'd come round to the front and kick you into the face. Most times he got my nose. I had my jaw broken twice with a kick, but I never got it seen to. I've a lump under my jaw now and I can really crack it.

The rows would start over silly little things. One time in the High Chaparral pub in Clogh, I was having a drink with my dad. A guy that I went to school with, who was home from England on holiday, happened to be in the pub. He came over and said, "Jayz, I haven't seen you for a long time. What are you doing now? Are you still at home or do you have a job?" Polite questions that a friend would ask you. I just passed the time of day with him. "No, I'm not working, I'm still at home."

Anyway, he went off and later on that night, when we got home, Daddy beat me with his belt and his fists. He said I was planning to run off with the guy. In the kitchen, there was £30 that Daddy had previously given me to mind because he had to pay a bill the next day. It was standing there, rolled up in a cup, not hidden away or anything. Daddy said I meant to use the money to run away, so he took it and burned it in the cooker.

I remember I was wearing a black dress that night with a silver leaf on the waist. Daddy tore it off me. He was wearing his cowboy boots and he kicked me with them.

On another occasion, in the late 1980s, we were

on our way back from a sheep mart. Daddy had been drinking heavily and was trying to strangle me as he drove along in the car. All of a sudden, he said to me, "I'll sort you out when I get home."

When we got back to Loon, I let the sheep out, put them into the field and pushed back the horsebox. He reversed the car in and then he started hitting me. He hit me with his belt and with a two-foot length of rubber pipe, which he used to use on the sheep.

I don't know exactly how it happened, but he tore off my shirt and bra. He broke the strap of my watch. Somehow he got off my jeans and wellingtons and socks. All I had on was just my pants. We keep a barrel under the barn to catch the rainwater and he stuffed all my clothes into that—the watch, the wellingtons, everything.

He kept hitting me with the rubber pipe and giving out that I was supposed to have been carrying on with the auctioneer at the mart. The man is married—I know his wife very well—and he had just been asking how was mother. I was saying mother was fine and he was politely saying, "Well, how's the sheep going? You haven't been in here for a while." I was simply passing the time of day with him, but Daddy had it in his mind that I would go with anything in trousers.

Anyway, after putting my clothes in the water barrel, he threw the house keys at me and said, "You can either stay here or walk home." He had another house key on the car keys so he could get in. He just took off in the van and drove home.

I waited at Loon for a long time. I didn't know whether mother might come up for me, but she never did, so I walked down through the fields. I was naked but for my pants. I couldn't walk the roads because all the car drivers would have seen me.

About three hundred yards from the house, I had to start walking on the road. I went round by the back of the neighbours' houses in case someone was looking out. My feet were bleeding by the time I got home.

It was very degrading. A couple of neighbours saw me go by in the distance. They could probably see I was almost naked, but afterwards they never said anything to me.

I wasn't badly hurt on that occasion, but I was admitted to hospital at least seven other times as a result of the beatings Daddy gave me. Mostly I went to St Luke's in Kilkenny and St Dympna's in Carlow. My mother would always drive me to the hospital, but never the night the incident occurred, always the next day when my father was sober. If she took me without his say-so, she'd get a beating when she got back home. I mean, he was the master in the house and he told you what to do.

He'd come up the next day and he'd look at you. "Oh Jayzus, you're hurt." If you were badly hurt, he'd send you to hospital or to a doctor. But he never said sorry. He'd say to Mammy, "You'd better get her sorted out."

I was admitted as an in-patient for various broken limbs, head injuries and concussion. I often had X-rays of my skull and other bones. One time I was admitted with black eyes and I told the doctors I'd fallen, but actually Daddy had been beating me. They kept me in overnight to see if there was any concussion.

The doctors would never really bother to ask me about what was going on, but if they did ask, I'd lie. When Daddy broke my wrist with the bar from the cooker, they asked, "Well, how did you do that?"

"Ah sure, I was playing football with the young lad and I fell." Some people have weak bones, so they probably thought I just had weak bones.

I don't think the doctors can be blamed for not doing anything to stop the abuse. The only people a lot of the blame falls on are social workers. And if they didn't have the power to help me, there wasn't a lot of good in their being there.

One time an accident happened to my mother through no fault of Daddy's. He was cutting down an ash tree and he was going to throw the trunk of it over the ditch. Mother was stood there and he threw off the trunk and, when it went down, whatever way it happened, the rest of the tree came up and split open mother's face.

When she went into hospital to get it stitched, they were all going on: "Did your husband do this?

Are you sure, now, he didn't assault you?" The doctors were all ready to get the gardai that time.

The pity of it is that, the one time the accident was innocent, the doctors wanted to take action. All the other times, when Daddy was beating me and I was too afraid to tell them, nothing was done.

9

ALCOHOL

*On Tuesday my father would sign on and on Thursday
he'd get his money. On Thursdays he'd go drinking in
Tom Reddy's pub in Castlecomer. He'd go in after
getting his money between 10am and 11am. He'd
leave the pub at around 3pm or 4pm. When he'd
come home from the pub, he always found an excuse
to start a row. Every time he got drunk, it meant that
I was going to get a beating. At the time I used to feel
that something I had done was causing the rows or
angered him. I don't really remember what started the
beatings, but they always started anyway.*

When we first came to Ireland, Daddy wasn't
drinking too heavily. He'd go out and have a couple
of halves and that would be it. But after two or
three years, it got that he'd have to have at least a
bottle of Powers whiskey a day. He used to drink in
Reddy's in Castlecomer, in the High Chaparral in

Clogh and in the Stonehaven in Carlow. Publicans used to love to see him coming, because he'd just stand there drinking money.

When he was signing on twice a week, he'd go in to 'Comer on a Tuesday and sign, then he'd go in on a Thursday to collect the dole money. He used to keep enough money out of mother's wages to drink on a Tuesday. Then, when he'd get his dole money on a Thursday, he'd drink again. He'd stay drinking until that was gone.

I used to get the £60 unmarried mother's allowance on Thursday too, and he'd have that drunk as well. When I came out of the post office, he'd be waiting and if I didn't give him the money, I'd get clattered there and then, in the middle of the street. People would look, then they'd turn away and walk off. The people in 'Comer just don't want to get involved in rows like that, yet they'll all talk about them afterwards.

At that time, Daddy would drink from, say, ten o'clock in the morning until closing time on Tuesdays and Thursdays, but then he wouldn't go drinking the following day. He'd buy drinks for everyone in the pub and most times he'd go off and leave money on the counter. One time he left £60 behind him on the bar.

At first, Daddy didn't drink at home, but then, after his father went into a home in 1984, he really started hitting the bottle. His father, Frank, had dementia. He could be happy as Larry washing up the dishes, then he'd put the teapot in the fridge or the milk outside the back door. He'd do silly little things and not even know he was doing them.

Eventually Granny Cooper had to put him into a home, for his own safety and for hers. She just couldn't handle it. But she never asked Daddy's opinion about it. He thought she should have done. Grandad died in the home in Devon a couple of years later. Daddy never went to see him before he died. The only time he went over was for the funeral. That was when Daddy really started drinking heavily.

He used to get poitin in vodka bottles at £5 a bottle. It was made by two old guys who lived some distance away—not in Castlecomer. One of the old guys, he's eighty-seven now, had great time for me. He's gone blind now from having cataracts, and they've given up making poitin, so there's no point in bringing them into it.

Daddy would go to buy the poitin on a Sunday afternoon, so there'd be nobody around to see him going. He'd buy at least eight or nine bottles. Then he'd drink some on Monday, go and get his whiskey in the pub on Tuesday, come home and drink on Wednesday, then go to the pub for his drink on Thursday and finally drink at home on Friday and Saturday.

Daddy was in court twice for driving offences connected with drink. One time, driving home from Carlow, Daddy was drunk and he went into a Merc. Mammy covered up for him and pretended she was driving. But there was a court case and they said the guy with the Merc was in the right, so we had to pay the costs of that case.

Another time, when we'd run Mammy into Braun to work, Daddy was driving and he was so canned, he couldn't even see which side of the road he was driving on. He drifted over the white line coming round a turn and smashed the wing mirror off a car coming the other way. He said to me, "What did I hit?" I said, "You're after hitting a car." He just put the foot down and drove like crazy until we got home. There was another court case and he had to pay two hundred and something pounds, on top of a fine.

Sometimes when he was drinking in the pub, if you said it was time to go, he'd turn round and hit you in the face and tell you to sit down and be quiet. He'd go when he was ready. But generally he didn't beat me in front of people; it was behind closed doors.

When he'd beat you at the farm, he'd think nobody was looking because it was so far off the road. But everything up there is so quiet that maybe a neighbour would hear the screaming and look out of his door. One neighbour did come down once, but when he saw me naked and Daddy beating me, he just went away again. I didn't see him at the time. He came to me afterwards and told me he'd seen it, but he said he was afraid to intervene. I feel he would have done something, but he didn't know what to do.

Our neighbours at the Deerpark must have heard
what was happening through the walls, but they
never tried to help. Daddy wouldn't let us talk to
them at all. They'd say "Hello" in passing, but after
you'd snubbed them enough times, they just got
fed up greeting us, so I knew it was no use running
in to them.

From 1987 onwards, Daddy was drinking the
whole time, though people only saw him drinking
on the two days he was in the pub. He used to
drink about two bottles of poitin a day, and he'd
drink it neat, without water. If he couldn't get poitin,
he'd get Mammy to go to the off-licence and buy
whiskey. When he was drinking at home, he'd start
at half-past six in the morning and drink all day.

He'd sit in a chair, watching telly, and start to
drink. He'd get up and turn that off when he started
to feel himself getting drunk. Then he seemed to go
back in time and talk about what he used to do
when he was younger and what his father used to
do and so on.

I've heard the same story about three hundred
times and each time it's different. He used to say
his mother never cared for him. But his aunts and
uncles have told me that Daddy's parents worked
their guts out to give him the best. All he would say
is, "They didn't care about me, they made me go
down to the beach and get driftwood for the fire,
they made me go fishing so they could have
something to eat, I had to scrub the floors." But his

family and schoolfriends told me this was all lies. He added different bits to the story or he'd change the date or the time. Mother was always at work at that time, Tanya had left home and Ben was in school, so I had to just sit and listen. I couldn't walk out of the room.

When Ben came in from school, Daddy would get down on the floor and roll around with him and play with him and then he'd hurt him and Ben would go out of the room crying. But still I'd have to sit there and listen to him. Eventually he'd fall asleep.

If he fell asleep in the chair, he'd be cranky when he woke up because he'd have a stiff neck. But if he was on the floor playing with Ben when he went to sleep, I could get a pillow under his head and cover him up.

If you could keep him warm and get him to sleep for five hours, then he'd stay asleep for a very long time and really sleep it off. But if he woke after two or three hours' sleep, he'd be bad-tempered and he'd start again.

Sometimes he'd get into his own bed, but you couldn't watch telly because the television was against his bedroom wall and the sound would wake him up. He was a very light sleeper, even when he was drunk.

I always used to think it was through drink that he began abusing me. But now that I look back on it, I think he had a problem all the time. Drink was just an excuse for the problem to come out.

We used to go regularly to the marts in Kilkenny and Carlow. We'd go to Kilkenny on Mondays and Carlow on Wednesdays. He'd show me how to buy and sell animals, who'd give you the best price, how to catch the auctioneer's attention without moving your hand, just by moving your eyes. It was useful information. It was one of the few useful things he ever did for me.

In June, July and August, we'd go to buy sheep. We'd have up to twenty sheep on the farm at once and we'd buy them four or five at a time. We wouldn't make a lot of money out of them—maybe £5 a head when we sold them. The farming was never very profitable.

Even when I was supposed to be at school, Daddy would take me to the mart. He'd buy the sheep, load them in the horsebox, then drive down, park outside the Stonehaven pub and go in and have a drink. He'd say it was bad luck to come out of Carlow without having a drink. I'd have to sit with him.

When he first took me to the pub, when I was seventeen or eighteen, he'd buy me Malibu or Stag cider or drinks like that. I'd drink whatever he bought me, but then I was getting drunk and that meant I'd get hurt worse from a beating. If I stayed sober I could avoid most of the blows. So I started drinking only minerals.

Daddy would stay in the pub until he got

absolutely drunk. Then, at seven or eight o'clock at night—or even later—he'd drive home. One night, when Ben was about four, we didn't leave Carlow until midnight.

When we got back to Loon, he was too drunk to reverse the horsebox into the barn. He said to me, "Get out, unload the sheep and push the horsebox back into the shed." I got out, opened the gates, unloaded the sheep and put them where they were supposed to go. I came back, unhitched the horsebox and pushed it back into its place.

"Now," he said, "I'm not able to drive, so you push the car back into the haggard off the lane." I was fierce winded, but when I'd finished he said to me, "Right, now you have to go and do your jobs while I sleep."

He got out of the car and got up on top of the bales in the barn and fell asleep. He had all his clothes on and a big, heavy coat on top. I thought that, lying on the bales, he'd stay asleep for a good while. When I'd done the jobs, I sat at the bottom of the bales, waiting for him to sleep it off.

The next thing he woke up and started shouting and roaring at me. Why was I sitting there? Didn't I know I was supposed to be in bed beside him? I was wondering what I was supposed to do. He was too drunk to listen to me.

This was the first time that he'd ever suggested I should be in bed with him or that he ever made me get next to him. He got down off the bales and started thumping and punching me. I just didn't know what to do. I stood there, and then he got me up on the bales and tried to rip off my jeans. He tore the zip, so I took them off.

Then he had sex with me. He never kissed me when he was having sex with me. He'd just get up on me. He never really said anything, just grunted. Afterwards he got my wrists and tied me to the string of the bales. They were the big round bales. Then he tied my feet to the bales and I was left there absolutely naked all night in the cold.

The next morning when he came up, he didn't say he was sorry or anything. He undid the string. He'd brought clothes with him and he threw them at me and said, "Get dressed now and do your jobs."

Another time, when I was about twenty-three, we went to the mart in Carlow and afterwards we went to the pub. A friend of Daddy's said to him, "My son is fond of Alison, would you mind if they went for a drink?" Father said, "Sure, they can have a drink here. I'll be talking to you. I won't mind." But the man said his son was barred from that pub and couldn't drink there, so could they go over to another pub across the road?

Daddy said that was fine and he told me, "You go, and behave yourself." I thought to myself, "What's going on? He's never let me off with a boy before." I knew there was going to be trouble at the end of it.

Anyway we went over to the pub and your man

bought me a drink. But he was only out after the one thing. He said to me, "How are you getting home? Your father will be gone home by now."

"He won't," I said, "He'll be in the pub waiting for us."

After one drink, I decided to go and see where Daddy was. I went over to the pub and his friend said to me, "Ah, he's gone home. You're to ring up when you want to go home." I said to the man I'd no money, and asked him to lend me twenty pence for the phone. "No problem," he said, "Give it to me next time you're in town."

When I phoned up, Mammy said, "OK, I'll tell him to come in for you. But you might as well start walking the twenty miles home." I could hear this noise in the background and I asked her what was going on. "Ah," she said, "Don't expect too many of your birds to be alive when you come back."

I loved my birds. I had about fifteen of them. There were canaries, siskins, there was a goldfinch and a chaffinch. Daddy had bought me the first one—a yellow canary—a couple of years earlier as a birthday present. I got some special birdfood which turned him red and he won second prize in a local show. One year I had twenty birds and put seventeen of them in for a show, but I was just pipped for a prize because the judges found that one little feather that should have been straight was curled.

Daddy and Grandad Scott had built the little lean-to where I kept the birds. It was the only time Mammy's father had ever come to Ireland. It had a long bench along one wall and that's where I kept the birds' breeding cages. I trained some of the birds to come and sit on my finger. One of them, Cheeky, a yellow, brown and white cross, would sit up over a press in the kitchen. When I'd look up at her she'd stick out her tongue at me. She could even talk to me.

Anyway, that night, while I was in the pub, Daddy went into the lean-to and opened up all the cages. He took out the birds and strangled each one.

When he arrived in Carlow to pick me up, he said to me, "Why did you go off with your man? You're only looking for the thing every other woman wants. You're no good."

In the car he said to me, "Jayz, you know what? That little bird of yours, the one you had trained, she sang to me while I had my hands around her neck, killing her."

When we got home he said to me, "Get out and clear up that mess out there." I went into the lean-to and found all the little dead bodies along the bottom of the cages. There were feathers everywhere because the siskins and the goldfinch were very nervous and he hadn't been able to catch them. That really hurt. I cried for the first time. I didn't cry in front of him, I went into my bedroom and cried. I never kept birds again after that.

Another time, Daddy got the chance of getting an Alsatian-labrador cross bitch. We'd always had an Alsatian dog as a guard dog. He said he'd make money by selling off the pups. There was one pup there, Bob, that no one else could do anything with. He wouldn't come when he was called or do what he was told. I just got friendly with him and he'd do anything I asked him to.

One day, there were fourteen or fifteen pups let out together. Daddy was shouting at me so Bob went for him and bit him on the leg. He didn't break the skin or anything, but Daddy got a slash hook and hit him right in the middle of the head. He opened his skull. You could even see his brains through the bone, the hook went that deep into him. But the dog lived. Daddy said that he'd tried to kill Bob, but he wouldn't die so he deserved a chance. He gave Bob to someone else.

Another time, I had a lovely little sandy brown Alsatian, the smallest of the litter. Daddy was sharpening sticks for the fencing. He had the points pared like a pencil. There was a row and the dog went for him. Daddy threw a stake at her and got her right between the ribs and killed her. After that, I didn't bother any more. I'd do my jobs but I wouldn't get attached to the animals.

Now I have a dog at home, a collie cross, which I got coming up to Christmas 1991. She hates Daddy. She wouldn't go next nor near to him. She had more sense than that.

10

THE BEATINGS
CONTINUE

In May 1990, there was a cow in a field at Loon who broke through barbed wire to get to a calf in a house and her teats were very badly cut. I was milking the cow when Daddy arrived. He started to get angry. I told him what happened to the cow and he told me I was lying. He started hitting me with his hand and then with the army belt, which was leather with a big buckle on it. After he hit me for a while with his belt, he started hitting my fingers with the hammer. He made me put my hands out palm down and he hit them with a hammer. Every time he hit me with the hammer, he said I wouldn't touch anything again for a while.

When Mammy was working the day shift at the factory, she and Daddy used to get up at five o'clock and make a cup of tea. Daddy would drive her over to work and come back with the van.

At the time, instead of keeping the poitin at Loon, he had it down in the house at the Deerpark. Whatever time he came back on this particular day, maybe around six o'clock, he started drinking. He came down at half-past seven and woke me up. He'd never come into the room when I was asleep. He'd always knock on the door, open it and shout at me. It would only be when he wanted sex that he'd come straight in.

I didn't get up until eight o'clock. That was plenty of time to get the young lad up for school. I looked at the poitin and saw there was half a bottle gone, so I knew that Daddy was fairly well on at this stage.

I got the young lad up and was getting him ready to go to school. About ten to nine, Daddy fell asleep on the floor, so I put the pillow in under him, got two blankets out of the press, covered him up, left the van keys there and walked up to the farm at Loon to do the jobs.

By this time, it was too late for the school bus, so I took Ben with me. Usually the jobs are done about half-past nine or a quarter to ten, but it was half-past eleven before I got up to the farm.

We had a cow who had calved at the time. She was supposed to be in one field, but, because I was late, she'd broken through three different fields to try and get to her calf in the shed. All her teats were cut by the barbed wire.

Ben went up and unlocked the shed and I went

and opened the gate for the cow and brought her down. I went to have a look at the hole she'd made in the fence, then I fed her and, while she was eating, I put the calf sucking.

Then I started to milk the cow while she was still eating. That should have kept her quiet, but she was so sore from the cuts, she wasn't willing to be milked. Even when the calf was sucking her, she was kicking.

I did what I could, but I gave up half-way through as she wasn't giving the milk down because she was so sore. Next thing, Ben comes running in. "Daddy's here! Daddy's here!"

Daddy left the van in the lane because he was still drunk. He said to me, "Bring the van in. Why is there no water up here?" We used to bring water up to the farm in tubs for the animals. "Sure, you were asleep," I said.

"You could have filled the tubs and put them in the van," he said. He went into the barn. "What's she done to my cow?" he said. He sat down to milk her and she kicked him. Then he saw the cuts on her teat and thought I had deliberately cut her with a knife.

He started shouting and roaring at me. "OK," I said, "you drunken bastard. You don't believe me. Come here and look at the hole in the fence." I was getting fed up with him at this stage. No matter what I did, I was always in the wrong. And I hated to see the way this cow was. She was really cut.

He grabbed up a slash hook and said sulkily, "Show me where the hole is, so." Walking down to the fence, he said to me, "Now, if you're lying, I'm going to cut your head off."

I showed him the hole and he said to me, "Right, get into the shed and do the rest of your jobs and clean up."

As I turned round to walk away, he caught me with the hook. All around my side was cut. I managed to walk back down to the shed and was going to let the cow out into the field to get a drink of water after putting stuff on her teats to keep the flies off. But Daddy followed me in.

"Come here," he said and he sat me down on a chair we always keep in the shed. He started ranting. I didn't listen to what he was saying. I knew by his actions when he was going to hit me, but I just turned off whenever he started shouting at me.

The next thing, he pulled me up, spread my palm out on the table and hit my hand on the table over and over again with a really heavy hammer. It was the hammer he used for doing the stone wall. He just kept hammering my fingers on both hands. As he hammered my fingers, he said I wouldn't touch anything of his for a long time.

I just stood there screaming with pain. He wasn't doing it lightly. He was vexed and was really hammering hard. Ben was peeping around two tar barrels to see if I was getting badly hurt. He was afraid, but he still watched the whole time.

When my father finished hammering my fingers, he got into the van and drove off.

I let the cow back into the field and I said to Ben, "Come on, lock up." We took the keys and I said, "That's it, I'm going and I'm never coming back."

This was about three o'clock. We went up the fields to hide in the shed of a neighbouring farmer, Matt Buckley, who I thought would help me. He's dead now. He had land further up the road and he used to walk up past our house every day of the week. One time he said to me, "Jayz, one day I'm going to find you dead up here. This carry-on is not right." I knew he'd be up the following morning and he'd bring food for us and would help me out.

We were hiding in his shed when, about ten past nine, Daddy came looking for me. Ben was crying and I couldn't stop him because he was hungry. Daddy heard him and found us and brought us home. When we got there, he beat me again with his fists and his belt. I couldn't defend myself because my fingers were smashed. I couldn't even feel them below my wrist. He punched me in the face and I got a broken nose that time.

He didn't let me have the fingers seen to afterwards. It was only a couple of months later when I couldn't bend one of my fingers—it would go blue with the cold, almost as if it were broken—that I went to St James's Hospital in Dublin. They told me the nerves in the finger were damaged and that it would never get better. The other fingers knitted back crooked. Now I get fierce pains in my fingers in the frosty and snowy weather.

That wasn't the only time Daddy acted crazy at Loon. I remember one really, really hot summer's day back in 1991. I'd been in Loon all day. Daddy and Mammy had left me up there at half-past nine. Ben had gone to school. I'd let the ducks and chickens out of the tin shed; otherwise they'd have smothered on such a hot day.

Anyway I was lying around in the sun, reading a book and minding the chickens, in case a fox would come and take them.

About half-past four Daddy drove up and said, "Matt Buckley is coming in a few minutes to bring up the bales of hay and stack them up. You give him a hand."

When Matt arrived, I went over to him and told him where Daddy wanted him to put the bales. Matt knew the field as well as we did and he knew there was only one place to put the hay. We were planning to leave the bales in the field all winter and Matt knew where the water hung, so he put them where they'd stay dry.

Daddy had left by this time. Matt started work and, when he had a good number of bales stacked, Daddy came back and told Matt he was putting them in the wrong place.

Then Daddy started setting fire to them. Every time Matt brought up more bales, Daddy would set fire to those too. All told, there were forty-eight round bales burned. Eventually Matt got down off his tractor and said, "What's wrong?"

Daddy said, "You're putting them in the wrong place. I want them over there." By this stage the forty-eight bales were well alight.

Matt didn't want to contradict Daddy. He'd seen the beatings before and he was an older man—he was about sixty-two. He wasn't going to interfere or he'd get a clout, so he said, "I'll be back tomorrow. You tell me then where you want the bales put and I'll stack them."

Daddy turned round to me and said, "Come on, I'm going for a drink."

"I can't go," I said, "all the chickens and ducks are still out."

"To hell with them, the fox can take them. I don't care."

I'd only have got another beating if I hadn't gone, so we went up to Clogh to the High Chaparral. He was telling people in the pub, "I'm going home now to burn my hay, the rest of it. I don't want any of it. There's going to be no animals left. I'm going to kill them all." None of them thought he was serious.

The hay Daddy burned that night was worth almost £600, and we hadn't even paid the contractor. It was just stupid really.

11

RUNNING AWAY

*When I was nineteen years old I told [a doctor], that
my father was having sexual intercourse with me. [The
doctor] called my parents in and Daddy walked out
half-way through the meeting. The following morning
I packed our bags and went. I took Ben to a hostel in
North Brunswick Street, Dublin. Later that year, I ran
away to England. I went to my grandmother's and I
was only there a couple of days when Daddy turned
up. When he got me back from England he beat me
very badly with the belt of his trousers and his hands
and he had sexual intercourse with me in my bedroom,
twice in two hours. I knew it was going to happen
after the row, so I didn't try to fight with him. All I
wanted to do was kill him but he made me so afraid.*

When I was about eighteen or nineteen, I decided
I couldn't stand the abuse any more and made up
my mind to run away. I borrowed some money

from a friend and went to Devon and stayed at the house of an old schoolfriend.

This friend had been at school with me in England and we'd kept in touch. He used to write to Granny to find out how I was, and I'd see him when I went over to Granny's for Christmas.

I turned up at his mother's and just asked if I could stay the night. I said, "I've a few problems and I've nowhere to stay." She said, "Would you not go down to your granny's?" But I said, "No, it's too late, I don't want to upset her. I'll go down in the morning."

But the next day Daddy phoned a friend in the village to see if I was there. When he came to get me a week later, he knew exactly where I'd stayed, who I'd been with.

I was in a pub playing pool with a group of friends when Daddy arrived. He said, "Get out, you whore. You're not staying here on your own."

He didn't hit me while we were at Granny's, but on the way home, I was terrified of what he was going to do.

When we got back to Carlow station, Mammy and Ben were there to meet us. Mammy asked if everything was OK. Ben was holding onto me. He was nearly in tears, but he was afraid to cry because Mammy kept looking at him. He asked me why did I leave. Did I not like him? That made me feel even more guilty.

When we got home, we had tea and scones, but

I couldn't enjoy them. The scones tasted like cardboard. I knew there was something coming, but I didn't know what to expect. Mammy said she had to go and see someone, and Daddy told her to take Ben with her.

When they left, I got a fierce beating. He just started shouting at me. Why had I left home? Was I not grateful for our happy house? I should have been grateful for having a roof over my head and being fed. He hit me with his fists, and on the back with his belt. I was lucky it wasn't on the face or chest. He beat me until my whole back was black and blue. He tore off my shirt and stubbed cigarette butts on my chest. I thought I was really hurt, that he'd broken some bones, but after a couple of days, the pain went away, so it must have been just bruising.

After a while, he seemed to lose his energy and get tired, so he pushed me into my bedroom, locked the door and went off to his own bed. He didn't sexually abuse me. I got undressed, got into my nightshirt and went to bed. Some hours later, Mammy came back and unlocked the door. She took me into the kitchen and I got a bit of tea and toast, then went back to bed.

The following day he said nothing to me about running away. He just acted as if everything was perfectly normal.

Some time later that year I told Daddy I was going to see a friend and went to see a doctor. I just went in on the off-chance that he could do something about what was happening. I wanted to stop the sexual abuse more than anything.

I told him that my father was abusing me and that I'd had a child for my father. The doctor didn't examine me; he just talked to me. He said, "I can't exactly do anything until I talk to your parents." I asked him, "What can I do? If Daddy finds out I was talking to anyone, I'll get a beating. I don't know what to do. I'm scared."

He said, "Leave it with me and I'll see what I can do. I'll get back to you." I gave him a friend's address to write to me, because Daddy used to read my post. But I got no letter and I was wondering what was going to happen.

Then, all of a sudden, one day Mammy got this letter saying, "Would Mr and Mrs Cooper please call to see the doctor. An appointment has been arranged. Please acknowledge it."

When Mammy came back from the appointment, she said the doctor told them I'd been in and he said he'd had a complaint that I was being sexually abused and physically assaulted and that my child was fathered by my father.

Daddy said, "That's not true," and walked out. The doctor said to mother, "Please do something about this. It's a serious offence. Your husband won't talk to me, so there's not a lot else I can do." Daddy came home and started drinking poitin and there was a blazing row. He said to Ben, "Your mother wants to have me put away for life."

Mother covered up for me by telling Daddy that the health nurse who visited Ben had told the doctor about me, and that I hadn't said anything. But still he wouldn't talk to me.

The following morning, Mammy and Daddy went up to Loon at half-past seven. There's a bus to Carlow from Castlecomer at half-past eight, so at twenty past eight, I had my bags packed and was ready and waiting for the bus.

The day I was in Carlow visiting the doctor, a friend had recommended that I visit the social welfare place. I asked a social worker there whether she knew of any places women could go to.

She told me about a hostel for battered women in Dublin and asked why I wanted to know. I said that I was just thinking about it, but I'd have to be sure that there was a place available. She said, "Well, I could ring now and see," but I said I didn't want a place immediately, though I might want one in the future.

In the end, I went up to Dublin to the hostel without even ringing to see if there was a place for me. I brought Ben with me. The people at the hostel were very nice. They asked me why I'd left home and I told them. They said I could stay and they'd sort out money for me.

When I arrived, they gave me a pan loaf, butter, milk, sugar, tea or coffee, something to have right away. They were very good. I was going to apply for the lone parent's allowance up there and stay at the hostel until I'd calmed down and sorted myself out.

We were up there two or three weeks and then Daddy found out where I was. I still don't know how he found out. Even Mammy didn't know where I was. He sat outside the place for three days in all weathers, harassing the other women going in and out. He was peeping into prams to see if Ben was in there. Eventually they had to ask me to leave. I had nowhere to go so I had to go back home.

We went home on the train and when he got me back, things were worse. Mammy took Ben and she cuddled him, but I really got a hammering that time. He was beating me around with his belt and a piece of rubber pipe which he'd brought down from Loon and which he used to hit the sheep. He was hitting me across the back and head with that.

After a while, he took me down to my bedroom. It was near enough the same as all the other times. He'd torn all my clothes off in the row. He just stood there looking at me with hate in his eyes because I'd run away. I thought it was because I'd taken Ben.

He pushed me down onto the bed and got up on top of me and ejaculated. He kept hitting me around the face and chest while he was ejaculating. It was the worst sexual assault he'd ever inflicted on me.

I could feel my lips swelling up and bleeding as he hit me round the face. I was trying to cry and I couldn't. He just couldn't care whether he hurt me or not when he was pushing himself inside me. Then, after he'd ejaculated, he went up to the kitchen to Mammy and locked the door behind him so I couldn't get out.

I thought, "Ah, lovely, it's finished," and turned round and got into my bed but within a couple of hours he was back down again and sexually abused me a second time, the same as before. This time I had a nightdress on. He didn't tear it, he just pulled it up. He kept hitting me even more the second time. After he'd finished, he just turned round and said, with real hatred in his voice, "You'll never run away again." Then he walked out of the room, without locking the door.

I felt that, whatever I did, I was destined to stay in that house. There was nothing or no one who could help me. Every time I tried to fight against him or protect myself, I just got knocked down. I was getting to the stage where I couldn't fight any more.

The first time I'd run away from home, I thought the reason my father had battered me so badly afterwards was because he wanted Ben. I was getting completely fed up. I thought to myself, "If he wants Ben, fine, he can have him." So after a couple of months, I ran away again to Granny Cooper's house in England. This time I left Ben behind.

Daddy had been watching me the whole time to make sure I didn't escape. But ever since 1987 or

1988, when he'd started drinking heavily, I used to take small change from his pocket when he was drunk. I'd take maybe a pound at a time. I had it saved up in the post office until I had £21.

I was supposed to be going shopping with a girlfriend. When I got to town, the girlfriend didn't turn up. Well, I wasn't going to give up a day's freedom. I had my post office book in my hand and I went into the post office in Kilkenny. They put the interest on the money, so it came to £25. I had another five pounds in my pocket.

I got the train down to Waterford and the train from there to Rosslare. The all-in-one single ticket, including the train from Kilkenny to Barnstaple in Devon, was £21. I had a few pounds left over for the bus fare and to get something to eat on the boat.

When I got to Granny's, I looked an absolute mess. She said I looked horrible, as white as death. I told Granny I'd had a row with Daddy, that I'd run away and was never going back.

On a previous occasion I'd told her Ben was her grandson. "I know he's my grandson," she said.

"Yes," I said, "but your son is his father." She wouldn't believe me the previous time, but this time, when I told her everything that had happened, she did believe me. She said, "Do whatever you can, but make sure he gets punished for what he's done to you."

Later that night Daddy phoned up and he said

to Granny, "Do you know where Alison is?" Granny said, "No, sure how would I know where she is?"

So then Daddy put Ben on the phone. "Where's Alison? I want Alison. I'll die if I don't get Alison. Where is she?" That really broke my heart, but still I said to myself I wouldn't go back. Daddy had Ben and I thought that's all he wanted.

I don't know whether he then telephoned a friend in the village or what, but somehow he found out I was at Granny's.

I didn't know he was coming. It was three or four days later and I was up having a bath at Granny's. Suddenly I heard him shouting downstairs, "Where's the bitch? I'll get her."

Granny said to him, "You're not to start trouble in this house. I know everything you've done. She's told me. If you start any trouble now, I'm going to get the police." He said, "Oh I'm not starting any trouble at all. Don't think that for a minute, mother. I just want to bring her home where she belongs. She's after putting that little fella Ben through hardship. He's at home crying. He wants his mother."

Daddy came up to the bathroom, but I'd already got out of the bath and dressed. I'd opened the bathroom door, because I knew if it was locked, he would have just kicked it in. He just said to me, "You get your things. Be ready to leave first thing tomorrow morning. We're going home."

That night I said to him I couldn't go home

because I only had a one-way ticket. So we went into the travel agents' before we went home the following morning and the man told us my ticket was a return ticket. The girl in Ireland had obviously made a mistake, so luckily enough I got home on that ticket.

Daddy didn't say anything on the whole journey back. It was almost as if you were travelling with someone who couldn't speak.

When we arrived home, he just told me to get to bed. He said, "You know what to do." So I stripped and I got into bed and then he came down and he said, "Get outside the bed," and he had full sex with me again. I didn't struggle this time, because I thought, "I've already run away so many times and been caught. I'm never going to be able to escape. I might as well just try and make the best of it." I just felt totally defeated.

1 2

THE PHOTOGRAPHS

When Ben was very young, my father got mother to get a Polaroid camera. He told me one day to go into his bedroom and he told me to strip and lie on the bed. I did and I was naked. He told Mammy he wanted photographs and she was to take them when he said so. Mother said nothing. When he got into the position he wanted, that is when he was licking my vagina, he told mother to take the photograph. She couldn't. She just stood there looking. Then he got up and started beating her. He hit her eyes and then he told her to take it again. This time she took the photograph. Then he got up and gave me the camera and told me I was to do the same.

A good few years ago, when Ben was only a baby, Daddy came into the kitchen one day and told Mammy to get her Polaroid camera. It had been a present to her from relatives.

She got it and he told us, "Come on into the bedroom, the two of you." When we walked in, there was a white bedspread on the bed. I'd never seen it before.

Mother said, "What do you want a photograph for?" And he said, "Well, what if one of you dies? I want to have a photograph to remember you by." I thought, "What's going on here? Is he going to kill me or has he something planned?"

We didn't know what was going on. After all, I had a good few family photographs taken already. So Mammy said, "What exactly do you mean?" And he told her, "I want photographs of the two of you naked."

He was stripping as he was talking and he said to mother and me, "Get them off." We took our clothes off and he said to mother, "I want you to take a photograph of me and her together."

He pushed me on the bed and pulled me so that my legs were up in the air and my bottom was right on the edge of the bed. The way it was, he pretended that he'd been licking me. He wasn't actually touching me, but in the photograph it looked as if he was.

Mammy wouldn't take the picture. She just stood there and every time he said, "Take the photograph," she just couldn't. So he went over and belted her in the private parts and on the chest and in the face with his fists. "Now," he said, "you little bitch, take the photograph."

I was just lying on the bed at this time. I was afraid to move because I saw what Mammy was getting. I was frightened that if I didn't do what I was told, I'd get the same.

He got back into the same position and she took the photograph. Her eye was cut where he had hit her and she couldn't really see what she was doing. Luckily enough the photograph came out.

This was the first time that my mother had actually seen my father sexually assaulting me. She had known it was going on, that he and I were down in the bedroom together, but this was actually the first time the three of us had been in the bedroom together.

Then Daddy told me to get up off the bed and mother had to lie down. He showed me how to use the camera and told me he wanted pictures taken of him and mother. I took photos of the various positions. There was one where she was sucking his penis. There was another where she was on the bed and he was up on top of her with his penis fully inside her. There was another photograph or two, but I don't really remember what positions those were.

There were five photos taken altogether, though only one of me. Afterwards, he just said to me, "Leave the camera on the dresser and go on about your business. I don't need you any more." I picked up my clothes, walked out and shut the door behind me. I went straight to the bathroom, ran a hot bath and tried to clean myself. I had felt his hair brush against my leg and I just wanted to scrub myself. He made me feel so dirty.

I stayed in the bathroom for half an hour. When I came out, their bedroom door was still closed, so I just took a book and went into my bedroom. They stayed in their bedroom for well over an hour—nearly an hour and a half. Nothing was ever said but I presumed they had full sex.

At the end of that time, my mother came down to my bedroom. She didn't really say anything, but it looked as though she'd been crying. Her eyes were still swollen. She borrowed some make-up from me, the brown powder, and she just tried to cover up the bruises as best she could.

This never happened again. It was the only time. I didn't see the photographs for a long time afterwards but last year, when we were cleaning out Mammy's bedroom, we found two of them at the back of a drawer. They'd slipped down behind the back of the drawer. I handed them in to the gardai as evidence—the one of him licking me and the one of her sucking his erect penis.

Daddy never mentioned this to me afterwards. It just happened and that was it. I felt dirty and cheap afterwards. I knew, after all this time, that it wasn't right but there wasn't a lot I could have done to stop it. I really felt used.

13

THE GARDAI

On Friday 6 December 1991, my father was in the pub drinking for a long time and I was with him. We went home early in the afternoon and a row started over going to England for Christmas. All of a sudden he started lashing out at me. He hit me with his fist and his belt. He also threw an electric kettle at me. Myself and mother were going out the door and getting into the van when he threw the carving knife and what was left of the kettle at the van. I rang the gardai in Kilkenny and told them I was a neighbour and that there had been a row in Coopers' and would they come out because I thought someone might have been hurt.

People have asked why I didn't report Daddy to the gardai for beating me and abusing me. Well, I tried on a few occasions.

Sometime in 1986, Daddy had stripped me down to my bra and underpants during a beating. While he was beating you, he'd tear at your jumper or shirt. He had one hand beating you and the other tearing at your clothes. You couldn't really stop him tearing your clothes, because your two hands were up trying to defend yourself. Normally I'd wear wellingtons without socks around the farm, so I wouldn't be wearing shoes or socks in the house.

This time I just felt I'd had enough of the beatings and I ran out of the house. I was almost naked and in my bare feet. I was going to hide in the garage but he went out and got a pitchfork and came after me. So I ran up the road to a friend's house and went in and asked if I could use the phone to ring the gardai.

My friend's mother said to me, "You've nothing on. You'll catch your death of cold. What happened you?" I told her what had happened, that there'd been a row and he'd stripped me and wouldn't let me back in. She said to me, "OK, ring the gardai," but we couldn't get hold of them; they were engaged.

Then mother came up in the car looking for me, so I ran out, got into the car and we drove off. She had clothes in the car for me. We went up to Loon and stayed up there for two or three hours. When we went back home, he was in bed and asleep.

Another time, the gardai actually did come out. Friday 6 December 1991 seemed like any other day. We went up to Loon and did all the jobs. Everything seemed fine.

Daddy had got his dole cheque through the post

and we went into 'Comer to cash it. Afterwards we went into Tom Reddy's pub and Daddy was drinking whiskey.

It had been arranged a week or so earlier that I would go to grandmother's in England on my own, just for a week's holiday, so that she wouldn't be on her own at Christmas. I didn't actually want to go, and I'd said so to mother. "Let Daddy go on his own, I want to be with Ben for Christmas." But, no, they said I had to go.

By this time I'd just got used to the idea that I was going. But it must have been festering in Daddy's mind because, after a few drinks, he started saying that we wouldn't let him go to England on his own, that we didn't trust him.

I said to him, "You can go if you want. I don't want to go."

"No," he said, "you have something planned over here. I'll go and you can come with me."

Nothing else was said in the pub at the time, but when we got home, Daddy started saying that mother didn't trust him and that she was carrying on with other men and just wanted to get rid of him and that I was the exact same. He said none of us cared about him—we just wanted him for his money.

He got really vexed then and started hitting us around. He hit me first with his belt and with his fists. Then he started on mother. At this time I was over beside the sofa, next to the door. There was a bit of shopping on the table—peas, beans and so on—that mother had got for supper that evening. He picked up the tin of peas and threw it at me. I dodged it and it went straight through the window.

This vexed him even more. He really got angry then. He said he wouldn't leave me off with that; I was going to get the beating of my life. I was really scared, so I ran out into the hall and down towards the bathroom. He came after me and started belting me and was there hitting me for a long time.

Then he went back up into the kitchen. The kettle had only just boiled and he threw the kettle of boiling water over Mammy. Fortunately she wasn't badly scalded because she had a jumper and a coat on; it got her on the back and the coat soaked up most of the water.

He said that's what I would get, so I had to put the kettle on and boil it up again so he could do exactly the same thing to me. When he picked up the kettle to throw the water at me, I ran out of the door, so he threw the kettle after me. When it hit the ground, it split in half.

Then he got even more vexed because I had dodged the tin of peas and the kettle. So he started throwing knives at me. He came out and picked up what was left of the kettle and threw that at me. Then he started hitting me with his belt. I don't know how long this was going on for.

Eventually he stopped and seemed to notice for the first time that the window was broken. He said to us, "Go up and get your man"—a neighbour who was a builder and plumber—"to come down and fix the window."

Mammy and I were getting into the car to go up to the neighbour's. My nose was bleeding and my face was all blood. I'd a cut on one arm where he'd caught me with one of the knives he'd thrown at me. As we were pulling out in the van, he came out and threw the remains of the kettle at the van and threw a knife at the van tyres to try and puncture them.

When we got to the neighbour's house, he was busy and said he'd be down in ten minutes. When we came home, Daddy was in the house. "Well," he said, "where is he?" Mammy said, "He'll be down in a few minutes, he's just getting a few tools together."

Daddy got out over the back fence and went up across the fields. I don't know where he went.

Your man came down then and we measured the window. He said to me, "Come on, have you money?"

"I've a small bit," I said.

"Between the two of us, we'll get the pane of glass," he said. This was around five or half-past five.

We went into 'Comer and got the glass. When we came back the van had gone and I thought mother must have taken it up to Loon to do the jobs. I went in to the house and Ben was there.

Mammy was in the bathroom. I said, "Where's the van gone?" She said, "Oh, Daddy's after taking it."

We got the window puttied in anyway. Your man said to me, "Will I drop you up to Loon?" but I said no, I'd hold on and see what was happening. I didn't want to leave Mammy there on her own in case Daddy came back.

I phoned up the High Chaparral in Clogh and asked the barman if Daddy was there. "Yes," he said, "but he's fierce beery. Will one of ye come up and get him?"

"No," I said, "we can't, because we've no car. And anyway, I don't want him knowing that I'm after phoning. Is there any way you could just keep an eye on him and ring the house when he leaves, so that we would have warning how bad he was and when he'd be back?"

While we were waiting, I phoned up the gardai in Kilkenny and said I was a concerned neighbour phoning about an argument in Coopers' house. I said I'd heard people screaming, that I was worried that someone might be seriously hurt and asked if they could please call out. I'd tried to phone the gardai on previous occasions, but this was the first time I'd actually got through to them. They said they'd try and get someone out.

About twenty minutes later, the barman phoned up and said, "He's just left." I said to Mammy, "What will I do? Will I go up to Loon to do the jobs or what will I do?" She said, "You'd better go up, because if you don't, you're going to get beaten for not doing the jobs."

It was dark and I was just getting ready to leave when the van arrived back. Daddy came in and started hitting me again. He said I was a bitch and that I should have done my jobs ages ago. He said he'd been up at Loon waiting for the past twenty minutes, but I hadn't come up.

I just stood there and let him hit me. I had a broken nose and I was really hurting from the first beating. The more I tried to fight him, the worse I had got hurt. It was almost as if my spirit was broken. I just couldn't fight any more. I just let him beat me.

About an hour later he stopped beating me. At this stage, I was standing naked in the kitchen, except for a bra and underpants. I had to sit there. There was no fire lit and it was fierce cold where the wind had been coming in the broken window before it was fixed.

He was talking away to Mammy, giving out to her. I don't know what he was giving out about. Ben was just sitting there in the chair looking at me. He hadn't actually tears in his eyes, but you could see that he was crying inside.

Around eight or half-past eight, Garda Tom Walsh arrived. He said a neighbour had phoned about a row. He could see that Mammy had a cut over her eye and I had a broken nose. Daddy was stood right behind the two of us. Garda Walsh asked Mammy first did she want to make a statement but she said no.

He turned round to me and said, "You're freezing. Why don't you go and put something on?" I looked at Daddy and he said, "Yeah, go on."

I went into the bedroom and I could just hear them talking. Tom Walsh said to Daddy, "What's happening, Michael?" And Daddy said, "Ah, these two just had a row. They were fighting and I stepped in and stopped them." But Tom Walsh must have known from the look of us that there hadn't been two women fighting.

I came back into the kitchen with a dressing gown on and the garda said to me, "Do you want to make a statement?" I said no. It would have been all right at the time making a statement to Tom Walsh, but the minute he was gone—and Daddy knew you'd made a complaint against him—he'd beat you even worse.

If Daddy had been taken away that night and kept overnight in the cells, then we'd probably have made statements against him, once we knew he wouldn't be back. We would have had the whole night to pack up our things and go to friends, or go somewhere.

But the way it was, Daddy would have beaten us worse. So we just said no—and hoped maybe things would get better. But they never did.

14

BUGGERY

During the summer about three years ago, my father had anal intercourse with me. I lay on my back and he grabbed my shoulders and turned me over so I was lying on my stomach and then he spread my legs with his hands. His legs were in between mine. His hands were on the bed beside my breasts and he kept forcing his way into my anus with his penis. He was hurting me very badly and I screamed out loud with the pain. He leaned on one hand and slapped me across the face with the other and told me to shut up. He ejaculated when his penis was in my anus.

One day in 1989, I remember I was working in the kitchen. Mammy was at work and Ben was at school. I was alone with Daddy in the house. He came into the kitchen and said to me, "I want a bit of sex."

I went into Daddy's bedroom and stripped. I kept my jumper and bra on but I was naked from the waist down. I lay lengthways on the double bed on my back, as I usually did. He undressed at the same time.

"No," he said, "turn over." I wondered what was going on, because he never did it any other way than with me on my back and him getting up on top.

I turned over and was lying on my stomach. As far as I was concerned, the quicker I could get it over with the better. The more I fought, the longer it took. I knew it was wrong, but it was less painful if I just did what he asked.

He got up on top of my back, spread my legs and put his hands on the bed next to my breasts. He put his penis between my legs and kept forcing his way into my back passage. I just screamed with pain. I couldn't stop screaming, but whenever I screamed, he just leaned on one hand and hit me across the face and told me to shut up. It lasted about twenty minutes. Normally it was over in ten minutes; it was never very long.

I could feel myself very wet afterwards and I didn't exactly know why. Whenever he'd raped me before, I was able to will myself not to respond, not to enjoy it, and I would be so dry that he hurt. I had been so young when he started abusing me, and the sex had been so painful, that intercourse had never been a pleasurable experience. I would imagine that I was away somewhere else and I would will myself not to respond to him. That's probably why he hurt me so much. So I couldn't understand myself being so wet.

When I got up, I noticed that there was blood on the bed. I knew that he'd had his penis in my anus, but I didn't know at this time that you weren't supposed to do that.

I went out and washed and put a sanitary towel on. But I continued bleeding and I had to put two sanitary towels on because the blood was coming through. The more I moved, the more I bled.

Later on that day, Mammy came home. The bleeding still wouldn't stop so I asked Daddy—in front of her—if I could go to the doctor because I was bleeding. Mammy said to me, "You shouldn't have your periods yet."

"Well, I've two sanitary towels on," I said, "and I can't stop the bleeding." I just looked at her, but she never said anything.

Daddy said, "No, you can't go. Stay here and just keep putting on sanitary towels. It will stop eventually. Don't worry about it." I don't know if Daddy told Mammy what he'd done, but I didn't. I was too sore and too hurt to say it to anyone.

I was bleeding for two or three days. I had to continue doing my chores. If I hadn't, I would have been beaten. But it was very, very painful working, bending over to lift a bucket of water or anything like that.

A couple of months later, Daddy went to do the same thing again. He told me to turn over onto my stomach. I remembered how much it had hurt the last time, but my spirit was broken and I just did as I was told.

I'd tried running away, I'd fought back, but the more I fought back, the worse I got hurt. So I just got onto the bed and turned over on my stomach, but then he said, "No, not that way. I could have done you permanent damage the last time. Just lie on your back and do it as normal."

I used to hate Daddy for the way he made me feel. I kept my hands down by my side and just clenched my fists. I wanted to hit him, but I knew that if I did, I'd only get hurt worse because he was on top and he had more power than I did. I just felt so horribly helpless.

I hated him so much that I just wanted to kill him. Soon afterwards, I thought I had my chance. At the time we had a good few sheep, and, for dipping them, we had a large bottle of sheep dip. It said on the bottle that, if the sheep dip was swallowed by humans, the person should be made sick immediately and medical attention should be sought. There were details on the side of the package telling the doctor in medical terms how to treat the patient.

The sheep dip was a sort of bluey-coloured liquid, but it went white when it was put into water. I put about two teaspoons of it in Daddy's Thermos. There was a small bit of a smell off it, but Daddy used to leave his tea to go cold before he'd drink it, and by then the smell was gone off it.

At the time, one of our cows was in calf and we were taking the milk from her for the tea. Daddy said it must have been the milk making the tea taste very "inky." I agreed that I got a small bit of a taste off it myself, but I said it wasn't too bad.

Every day he'd drink five or six litres of tea and into every cup, I'd put teaspoons of the stuff. I thought to myself, "Surely he must get sick, he must have a pain in his stomach, something." But he never did, he never got sick.

I wish now that I'd killed him. The way the prison sentence turned out, it wasn't long enough. But if he were dead, Mammy and I would have our freedom.

15

BLIND!

In 1991 my father and I went to England to stay with his mother for Christmas. On Boxing Day, all of a sudden, he wanted to go back to Ireland. He packed up all the bags, threw things into them and said we were going home. I tried to tell him there were no trains running but he didn't listen. We walked up past the village, up a hill. I was in front and he was behind and he was shouting. He kicked me in the back of the leg without warning and I fell down. When I was trying to get up he kicked me straight into the eye. He was wearing steel toe-capped boots. My eye started bleeding. I could feel the blood running down my face. I have only partial vision in my right eye now. I can only see darkness or light. I cannot make out shapes or anything.

Coming up to Christmas 1991, Daddy and I started making preparations for going to Granny's house in England. But before we left, we had to make sure all the work was done.

That year, we'd decided to rear some turkeys at Loon for the Christmas market. We had seventy turkeys all told and, on the Friday and Saturday before Christmas, we started killing them.

We'd kill the turkeys by hanging them up from a rafter by their feet, putting a knife in their throat and cutting the main vein in the roof of the mouth. The blood dripped down into a bucket. The turkeys would just close their eyes and within two seconds, they were dead. It was a more humane way of killing the birds than wringing their necks. For them, it was just like going to sleep.

On the Sunday we were due to go to England, Mammy had driven Daddy and me up to Loon. He'd been drinking poitín all day. We'd already killed fifty turkeys and there were twenty left to kill on Sunday morning. Daddy killed two of the birds but he made a mess of it because he was so drunk. I plucked those two and told him I needed another one.

Daddy said he couldn't kill the turkeys. "You'll have to do it," he said, "I can't even see." So I caught up the turkeys and started killing them two at a time. I had the twenty of them done by half-past one.

Mother had gone home with Ben to cook the dinner. We were supposed to have a roast dinner before we left. We'd worked it out that, if we had everything done by one o'clock, we could go down to the Deerpark, have some dinner, get washed and changed and be ready to leave at three o'clock. We had to be in Carlow for the bus at four o'clock.

Mother came up to get us but he started going on, "Hold on now, I have to look at my two cows here because of all the blood, to make sure they're all right." Most animals don't like the smell of blood and they get nervous and start kicking. Daddy went over to the cows and started soothing them. In fact, I'd already washed out everything with disinfectant so there was no trace of blood.

It was around a quarter to two when we were going home. Then Daddy had to have his dinner and get washed and changed. He was too drunk even to stand up and he cut himself several times while he was shaving.

Anyway, we went off and got the bus. Daddy poured what was left of the bottle of poitín into a small Club lemon bottle, so he could bring it with him on the bus. I had charge of the tickets. He gave me £50 for bus fares then, after taking a good few sups out of the bottle, he fell asleep.

When we got on the boat in Rosslare, he drank what was left in the bottle and threw it away. He slept during the four-hour boat crossing and he was a lot better tempered when he woke up. He acted as if it was just a normal day. He carried the two bags off the boat and onto the train and paid the train fares. By this time, it was about two or three o'clock in the morning.

We got to Granny's house about twelve o'clock the day before Christmas Eve. Daddy was well-behaved; he didn't start a row; he didn't argue. You'd think he didn't have a drink problem, the way he was carrying on.

He took us out that night—Granny and me—and we went up to the village pub. He had two or three pints—he can drink ale over there and it doesn't affect him—and half a whiskey, then we came home. We had a cup of coffee and went to bed.

On Christmas Eve, Daddy was fine too. I felt everything was so normal that it was abnormal. He hadn't been argumentative, he didn't try and pick a fight. To me, that wasn't normal. I knew there was something going to happen, but I didn't know what.

The following day, Christmas Day, Granny said to me, "Will he go for a drink?" I said, "I don't know." In Ireland, Christmas Day is a black day for Daddy because there are no pubs open, so we told him it was the same in England. Even though the pubs were open, we told him they weren't.

He was fine that day too. He sat down in front of the television. In the afternoon, we went out and put flowers on Grandad's grave, said a few prayers and walked back to the house again. This was too good to be true. Even when he was sober at home, he'd try to start an argument over something. But here he wasn't causing trouble; he was being very kind.

The following day, Boxing Day over there, we went up to see some of Daddy's friends. This was around half-past nine, ten o'clock in the morning. Your man said, "Come down to the pub and we'll get a drink." We'd told Granny we'd be back around half-past eleven. That was dinnertime to her, because she gets up around half-past seven in the morning and she always likes her dinner at twelve o'clock.

We were having a few drinks in the pub. Then I said, "Dad, it's quarter past eleven. We'd better be going down to Granny's now because she'll be looking for her dinner."

"Ah, it's all right," he said, "we'll have one more and then we'll go."

Around a quarter to twelve, Granny came up looking for him. She came into the pub and said, "Michael, what about my dinner? Will I have to cook it or is Alison going to get it?"

"Have a drink and we'll all go down together," said Daddy.

We had a drink. Granny doesn't really drink— she'll have maybe one glass of Bailey's and that's it. After she'd had her drink she said to Daddy, "Come on, I want my dinner, I'm hungry. It's OK for you. You're not used to breakfast or dinner. But I like my dinner. I'm used to it."

"OK, we'll go," said Daddy.

But then the lads we'd come up with started slagging him. "Oh Mary's looking for you. Sure, you're forty-seven years old and Mary has to come looking for you." It was almost as if he was a child again. That made him really annoyed.

When we were walking back to Granny's, we had to pass two other pubs. One of them he never goes into, he doesn't like the guy who owns it, but when we got to the other, he said, "Come on, we'll go in here just for one and then we'll go home." But Granny said, "No, you've had enough. They'll only kick you out. They don't like drinking like that in Mortehoe."

When we got back to Granny's, Daddy went in, slammed the door, went up to his room and got a £50 note and said to me, "You stay here and cook the dinner." I cooked the meal and had a bit myself. About an hour later, there was a telephone call from a pub. "Your father's up here drunk. Would you kindly come up and bring him home. He's tormenting some of the customers."

I went up to the pub. It was about four o'clock in the afternoon at this stage. Daddy ordered me a pint of ale, but I told the barman I didn't drink, so he put me up a pint glass full of orange. I drank it and said to Daddy, "Come on, we'll go home. I thought you wanted to watch something on television."

"Oh all right," he said, "come on, we'll go home."

I couldn't believe it was so easy to get him out of a pub. In Ireland, he wouldn't leave a pub and the more you tried to get him out, the more irritated he'd get. He hated being told what to do and it would really anger him.

We went down to the house and Granny said something to him. What it was, I don't know, but Daddy said to me, "Go in and ring up that train station. We're going home now. I want to know the times of the trains." But when I phoned up, I got an answering machine saying that no trains were running that day because it was Boxing Day. They'd be running the following day.

I went into the kitchen and told Daddy, but he said, "I don't care, we're going. I'm not staying where I'm not wanted."

So we packed up the bags. I was carrying the two of them. We were walking up a steep hill out of the village, planning to walk the fifteen miles to the train station in Barnstaple to catch a train the following day.

I was walking in front of Daddy when he kicked me in the back of the leg. I had the weight of the two bags on my shoulder and I went down. I was on my hands and knees beginning to get up when he came round to the front of me and kicked me straight into the eye. I fell back on the ground and he started pulling at my shirt. "Get up, get up you bitch. That's not good enough for you."

I could feel my eye bleeding. I couldn't see out of either eye and as I was getting up, I tripped over one of the bags and fell down again. I didn't actually see him taking off his belt, but he started leathering me with it. The more I moved, the worse I was getting hit.

All of a sudden I heard footsteps and a torch was shone into my eye. It was dark by this time. I could vaguely make out a face behind it. A man's voice said, "Jesus, what's going on here?" Daddy turned round and said, "Oh I caught this one with a fella and we're going home. We can't have her whoring around the town here."

"There's no need to beat her like that," said your man. "What have you done to her?" He said to me, "Do you want a doctor?"

I said, "Please get me a doctor. Take me somewhere so I can get a doctor." Daddy kept coming over to hit your man, but every time, the man would push him and Daddy would fall down, he was so drunk. In the end, the man said to him, "If you don't sit there, I'm going to give you a hiding, exactly like you've done to this girl."

All I could say was, "Please get me to a doctor." I knew I was hurt, but I didn't know how badly. I could feel my eye all swollen out. The man wanted to know where I lived, but I couldn't tell him with Daddy there. Daddy said, "We're Irish citizens and we're on holiday. If you want to take her to a doctor, go ahead. I'll tear up these tickets here and now." And he took out the boat tickets and was going to tear them up.

At this stage, the man just got fed up with all the hassle and walked off. He didn't say anything, he just disappeared. I didn't even hear him going.

Daddy got up and kicked me in the legs and said, "Come on, get up, we're going to Barnstaple."

So we walked on. I was seeing double. I was walking in the middle of the road and could see four lots of hedges. After about eight or nine miles, we reached a phone box and Daddy told me to go in and ring for a taxi.

I couldn't see the numbers. I was trying to read the taxi numbers off a list above the phone, but I was feeling faint and dizzy. Eventually I got through to a doctor's answering machine. I just put the phone down and told Daddy there were no taxis because it was Boxing Day.

"All right," he said, "we'll carry on walking." I just slumped to the ground. I couldn't walk. I was feeling faint and dizzy. I thought I was going to pass out. And I was still carrying the two bags; he wasn't carrying anything.

But he made me get up and we walked on, miles and miles. By this stage, Daddy had sobered up. Eventually, at the top of a hill, we saw a woman and husband in a car turning into her gateway. Daddy walked over to them.

"I wonder could you help me?" he said. "We've been mugged down the road. Three fellas mugged us. I held off two of them, but my daughter got badly beaten by the other one. I'd appreciate it if you could get us to a hospital."

As it turned out, the woman had gone to school with my mother. They were very kind. I still keep in touch with them. They took us into the North Devon Infirmary. At the hospital, the doctor put six stitches in the cut above my eye. They tried to stitch the bottom cut but it was too painful, even when it was numbed, so they just put cream on it. Every time I got up off the bed, I couldn't move, I felt so dizzy. All I wanted to do was be sick.

They took me back out to the waiting room. I sat with my head between my knees; that was the only way I didn't feel dizzy. Meanwhile, Daddy had filled in a form. He'd told the doctors the same story about being mugged. He said he'd hurt his ribs and he thought they were cracked, but not to worry about him, just to get me sorted out.

The receptionist asked where we were going to stay. Daddy asked if she knew of any good bed and breakfast places. "Yes," she said. "There are two good ones down the road which should be open. They'll take you in."

She got us a taxi and we went down to the bed and breakfast. But when they took one look at my eye, that was it. "Oh no, no, we couldn't have her in here. It's Christmas time. We don't want the hassle of washing bloody sheets," and all this.

At this stage, the effects of the anaesthetic were wearing off and I was actually being sick. Nobody would take us in. Daddy said, "I know where we can go," so we walked up the town to the train station. There were no benches, just the cold platform, so all we could do was go through our bags, get out our heaviest jumpers and put them on and lie back to back on the platform.

It was freezing cold. I hated the thought of even being near to Daddy, but to keep warm I had to lie back to back with him. I used my bag as a pillow. I still have it, covered in blood where my eye was weeping blood on it overnight.

The following morning, the first train came in at six o'clock and was cleaned out, before leaving at seven. We got on it. I can remember little children going to visit people on the Christmas holidays looking at me. "Oh look at that poor girl. What happened to her?" The same happened on the boat coming over.

When we got back, we managed to get a train to Waterford but there were no trains to Kilkenny. So we phoned Mammy. Daddy wanted her to get a neighbour to bring her down, because she's not very good at driving long distances.

I told her, "Get one of the neighbours to mind Ben. Whatever you do, don't bring Ben down with you." She went to see a friend who said, "Yes, I'll drive you down to Waterford, no problem." But there was nobody to mind Ben, so they brought him with them.

I was so grateful for a warm car. But when I got into the car and Ben saw my eye, he just started screaming hysterically. He was holding onto me and screaming. He couldn't stop. The poor thing, he just held onto me. I'll never forget that night.

When we got home, Mammy asked what had happened. Daddy just said, "Look what I did to her through drink."

On New Year's Day, I was to get the stitches out so I went to Dr Skuce. Mammy was with me and she told him I'd been mugged in England. The doctor examined my eye. "What can you see? Can you read the chart?" Stuff like that. I couldn't see anything so he sent me in an ambulance down to Ardkeen Hospital in Waterford. They did tests on me straight away, but they didn't ask how my eye was hurt. The ambulance waited for me and brought me home.

That week, I went back to Ardkeen four times and had laser treatments, catscans and other treatments. They asked me how the injury happened, but each time Daddy was with me, so I couldn't say anything. They said to me if I got a knock to the head, it could either bring my sight back or I could lose it altogether.

If I look at a light now, I can just see a blur of light, but apart from that, it's complete darkness. I'm almost totally blind in my right eye.

The following week, Daddy got drunk again and started saying to me, "Look what I've done to you. How do you think I feel?" But he never said he was sorry.

16

THE LAST TIME

My father was drinking poitín. He got very, very angry
and started hitting me with his hands and then his
belt. He asked me a question and when I didn't answer
he hit me with the vodka bottle and I felt a gush of
blood running down my neck behind my ear. After he'd
hit me a few times, he pushed me outside the door. I
heard mother saying, "You've hit her enough. Leave
her alone." When I heard her saying that, I thought
he was coming again, so I got out over the fence and
ran out over the back and lay in the long grass. I never
returned to my home in the Deerpark again until my
father was in custody in September. Since I left home
I feel much happier. I am not as afraid.

The last times I had sex with Daddy were on Sunday
12 January 1992 and again on the following Monday
or Tuesday.

On the Sunday, Ben went to bed between half-past seven and eight o'clock. Mammy went into his room to read him a story. I was in my own bedroom when Daddy came in.

He said nothing, just pushed me on the bed. I said nothing to him, I just lay there looking at him. He said, "Get them off," and I took off my trousers and underpants. He just lay on top of me, put his penis in my vagina and ejaculated. Afterwards I went into the kitchen, got a drink of water and then went to bed.

On the Monday or Tuesday morning, after Ben had gone to school, I was in the kitchen by myself. Daddy came in and said to me, "I want a bit of sex." He went down to my bedroom and I followed him. I took off my shirt, trousers and underpants myself, but left on my bra.

I lay on my back on the bed and Daddy got up on top of me, put his penis into my vagina and ejaculated. When he got off, I went to the bathroom and washed myself. We then went up to Loon to do the jobs—feed the animals and clean out an outhouse.

The following Thursday, 16 January 1992, Daddy had been drinking poitin all day. We were up in Loon doing the jobs, but decided to go down to the Deerpark to get Daddy's dole cheque because he had a few bills to pay.

It was about three o'clock when we got home, because Ben wasn't home from school. Daddy ate a sandwich and I thought if I could keep him eating, it might sober him up.

Then two lads arrived looking for scrap cars. I knew one of them from school. At this time Daddy had two scrap cars above in Loon. They offered him £20 down and £20 later if they could take the cars and all the rubbish from the farm. He said, "That's OK, but I want the two back axles to make a trailer."

If he hadn't sold the rubbish, he'd have had to pay £25 for a skip, so he was making money. Daddy told mother and me to go into 'Comer to get a few messages and pay the bills. He went up to Loon with the two guys. He was still drinking poitín, just to show off.

When he came back, Ben had arrived back from school. Daddy started saying I had something going on with one of the lads—the one I knew from school—and that was the only reason your man had come out to the house. The man had given Daddy £20, but Daddy put it straight into the fire. He said he didn't want dirty money.

Then he started calling me a whore and hitting me. He beat me with his belt, he beat me with his fist. He hit me over the head with a bottle and I could feel a lump which started to bleed.

During the row, a neighbour called to the house. Daddy pushed me into my bedroom and locked the door. I took off my jumper which was covered in blood and put on a T-shirt and jeans. Your man came into the kitchen and stayed for half an hour. They had tea. When he left, Daddy came down and unlocked my door. He seemed quieter, not as angry as he had been at first. "Come on up and get your cup of tea," he said.

I had only taken a mouthful or two out of the cup when Daddy started hitting me again. He poured the last of the poitín into the cup and said, "Every time I look at this, I'll think of what you did to me." I think he was blaming me because he had blinded me.

Ben was watching all this. Then Daddy pulled off my T-shirt and bra and pointed to my breasts and said to Ben, "Take a good look, son. This is the difference between a man and a woman." It was a very degrading experience for me and for Ben.

Then Daddy started hitting me again. He cut me on the arm so I had to have three stitches. He hit me with a salad cream bottle and broke my finger. He threw mugs, plates, knives at me. He made me sit on the chair and not move. He was ranting, but I wasn't really listening. He continued beating me with his strap. Then he produced a lighted candle and held it under my breasts. He had a cigarette and started stubbing it into my skin all along my chest. I still have the scars.

There was a fierce horrible look in his eyes—really, really horrible. I'd never seen it before. It was almost as if he was out to kill me that night.

When he had finished burning me, he told me to get another T-shirt. I just had a T-shirt, jeans and socks on. He pushed me out of the door and said,

"If you want to go whoring, I want the money. Go on, get the one who's going to pay the most."

Ben was sitting on the sofa watching all this. Daddy didn't seem to notice him there. While he was hitting me, that was all he focused on. He didn't even seem to realise when there was someone else in the room.

I went into the garage next to the house and stood there for about ten minutes. I could hear Mammy screaming at him, "You've hit her enough. Now leave her alone." When I heard this, I thought, "Christ, he's coming after me, I have to go."

I just got out over the fence and ran up the garden and lay in the tall grass. How long I was there, I don't know. I could even have passed out. I could hear Daddy smashing stuff in the house. The neighbours must have heard what was going on. On other occasions, they'd seen the cuts and bruises, but they didn't want to get involved. Since all this happened, they've told me they didn't realise it was as bad as it was. They said if only they'd known, they'd have done something to help.

All of a sudden, I saw a man hop over the wall and walk up the field. He stood at the top of the slope, silhouetted against the light, about four or five feet away from me. Although it was pitch dark, I thought, "If Daddy sees him, he'll think it's me stood there and he'll come up." I was about to get up and run when the man walked off in the opposite direction. To this day, I don't know who he was.

I got up and ran to a friend's house up the road. But when I looked through her window, I saw that she had neighbours in with her. A load of the local young lads were standing in the road outside. They told me Mammy had just passed them on her way up to Loon. One of them said to me, "What happened to you? You're wet and you're shaking."

I said, "Ah, I'm after having a row below and I'm not going back this time." The next thing one of the lads turned round and said to me, "What's your father wearing?"

"I'm not really certain," I said, "but he had a white jumper on. Why?"

"Well he's just after falling out of your gateway below. It looks as if he's coming this way."

I hid under a parked car so Daddy couldn't see me. He came up to the lads and asked if they had a light. They hadn't, but Daddy said it didn't matter, he was going up to Loon to do a few jobs.

Once he'd gone, one of the girls said she'd take me and get me cleaned up. But I said all I wanted to do was go and get a pair of slippers on—I had nothing on my feet at this stage—and see how Ben was.

When I went into the house, it was a total mess. There was broken delph everywhere, the table was upturned, there were smashed ornaments, chairs were broken.

We'd been rearing a few chicks beside the fire at the time, but they'd got hit by crockery and so on.

There were dead chicks all over the floor. He'd taken my jewellery box. I didn't have much but what little pieces I owned, he'd broken them and thrown the bits on the floor.

When I went into the kitchen, Ben was there in his pyjamas. He was trying to pick up the things that weren't too badly broken. I said, "I'm all right, son. You look after yourself and look after Mammy, and I'll see you tomorrow. Just tell Mammy that I'm OK and I'll see her tomorrow."

I had it in mind that I'd call her somehow. Ben said all right, so I said, "Be a good boy for me and get back into bed and tomorrow I'll let you know where I am and how you can reach me."

He said, "I'll save your little bits and pieces." Then he went and got back into bed and I gave him a kiss. He was crying so I told him, "Don't worry, it'll be OK."

I knew if I could manage to walk to a friend's house about four miles away I'd be all right. When I got there I tapped on the bedroom window. She came to the door and I don't remember going in. I just remember that I couldn't walk and I fell in the door. My friend was horrified. She washed my hair to see how bad the cuts were. But one of them was really deep and they couldn't stop it bleeding.

She took me into Dr Skuce in Carlow. He wasn't on duty but his partner, Dr O'Kelly, was. She stitched the cut on my head and took me down to St Dympna's to have my arm looked at and stitched.

But she couldn't stop my head bleeding, so she got an ambulance which took me straight into Kilkenny. They did X-rays of my skull and fingers, and they put a tight sort of cap on my head to stop the bleeding.

The doctor took a blood count and told me I must have only had about two pints of blood left in my body. He said the way my head was bleeding, within another two or three hours I would have died. I was really weak and drained. I didn't know what was going on around me.

The doctor examined me, took X-rays and then he took Polaroid photos of the bruises on my back, my chest, my legs and the stitches in my head.

I told him I'd been assaulted by my father, that he'd hit me over the head with a bottle during a row, and that I just wasn't going back home. At this stage I was fed up with all the lies. I told him exactly what happened, though I don't think I told him about the sexual abuse. I was in a state of shock at the time. When they asked me for an address for next-of-kin, I gave the address of the friend who'd driven me to the doctor's.

My friend stayed with me until I got into the bed in the ward at three o'clock in the morning. She said she was supporting me all the way, so I knew I had someone standing behind me. She'd known about the physical abuse and, though she had an idea about the sexual abuse, I'd never actually told her.

I assume my friend or the hospital called the gardai because at three o'clock that morning they went out to the house. Mammy was sat up in a chair reading, waiting for me to come back. Daddy was in bed asleep. Ben was still awake. He wouldn't go to sleep that night because he didn't know where I was.

The garda asked Mammy, "Is Mr Cooper here?"

"Yes," she said, "he's in bed. But please don't wake him. Why? What's wrong?"

"Do you know where your daughter is?"

"No, I'm waiting for her to come back."

Garda Luke Kelly, one of the gardai I later got friendly with, said, "Well, she won't be coming back. She's in hospital. You're very lucky that there wasn't a murder committed tonight."

Mother was really horrified and started crying. Ben came out to see what Mammy was crying about and, when he saw the gardai there, he started crying. Then Daddy was woken up by all the crying and he came out.

The gardai told him what had happened and he turned round to them and said, "Sure, I hit her a few times with my fist, but I didn't do her any damage. It must have been whoever she was sleeping with last night that hurt her."

The next day, my friend came into hospital in the morning and brought me clothes, a nightgown and so on. Mammy came in during the evening. She brought Ben in with her. He didn't want to leave at the end of the evening. He knew I was hurt and he wanted to stay with me, but Mammy took him home.

The following day, Daddy came in. I'd told the nurses I didn't want him allowed up to me, but I suppose that they just didn't see him coming in. I couldn't shout for the nurses because there was a woman in the next bed to me and she said, "Ah, isn't that nice, your Mammy and Daddy coming in to see you after your accident." The nurses had told the other women I'd been in a car accident.

"Right," said Daddy, "you're OK today. Now pack up your things and come home. Mammy will be in for you in about twenty minutes." With that, he just turned round and walked out. That really hurt. I thought he might have felt guilty about what he'd done, but he didn't.

Mammy kept coming to see me and telling me that Daddy said I wasn't to sign anything or make any statements. But I didn't take any notice. I'd made a promise to myself when Daddy blinded me at Christmas that he would never hurt me again. I didn't care how I was going to get out of the house, but I was going to get out. Daddy had hurt me badly this time, and this was my last chance of escape.

The social worker had been up to see me and told me that if I made a statement against Daddy, I could be placed in a home somewhere where I'd be protected. I said, "What about Ben? I have to get

Ben." She said, "That's OK. We'll just watch and when he goes to school, we can get him out."

When I was told that—and I knew that people were prepared to help me at last—I agreed to make a statement to the gardai.

17

THE FINAL HURDLE

The next morning Garda Agnes Reddy came down to see me in the hospital. I'd seen her once before when she came out to the Deerpark to try and persuade Tanya not to see her boyfriend. She asked me if I wanted to make a statement but I said no, I just wanted to be left alone.

Later on that day, Luke Kelly, another garda, came down. I felt I could trust him. He said to me, "Look, I can't help you, I'm not a bangharda. Your best bet is to talk to Agnes. If she can help you at all, she will. But the only way she can help you is for you to talk to her."

He said that, with my permission, he'd send her down to me. "Please," he said, "you don't have to talk to her, but if you do, it will help you a lot."

The first time Agnes came down, it just seemed like she just wanted to hear a complaint, but the second time she was more understanding and sympathetic. I found it easier to talk to her, but even then, I didn't tell her everything. I remember telling her about the physical assaults, but it was only later on that I told her about the sexual assaults. A couple of days later, I told her that Daddy was Ben's father.

She wrote out a statement and I signed it. She said she'd keep in contact with me. She organised a place for me in Oasis, a women's hostel in Waterford.

Agnes got my clothes out of the house—well, she got some of them because Daddy burned a lot of the others—and she got clothes for Ben. The day I left the hospital, the social worker took me to Ben's school at about ten o'clock in the morning. I took him out and the two of us went down to Waterford. Mammy came in to see me in the hospital at ten to two but I wasn't there. She got suspicious and phoned home to see if I was at home. Daddy guessed what was happening and said to her, "Go straight into the school and get Ben."

But by the time Mammy got to the school, Ben was long gone. She went out to Daddy and said, "He's gone," so Daddy went into the gardai and told them I'd kidnapped him. Daddy said he had adoption papers for Ben, but when the gardai looked into it, they said, "No, she's perfectly within her rights. It's her son." And Daddy started giving out and said, "Well, I adopted that child." Mammy had never told him that I didn't sign the adoption papers.

Meanwhile, I was settling in at the refuge in Waterford. It was very nice. You had your own room with bunk beds. You had a big table, four or five chairs, a kitchen unit, sink, cooker. You'd have a cupboard with all plates and stuff in it. But, while I enjoyed being there, all the time I knew Daddy was looking for me.

There was a man—Seamus Roche, who came from Waterford—who used to call to the house in the Deerpark with videos. His wife was a volunteer in the hostel and she used to tell me that Daddy was looking for me and he'd been talking about what he'd do when he found me.

She said Daddy kept asking Seamus whether he ever saw me around Kilkenny or Waterford or anywhere. He said if Seamus ever saw me, he was to go back and tell him. Seamus never did, but I was always looking over my shoulder. I was always afraid that he'd find me, that he'd turn up.

I didn't talk to Mammy for six weeks after I left home, but she phoned Agnes. "I want Alison to ring me. Get Alison to ring me, please, I'm worried about her." Actually, I'd sort of made up my mind that I would contact her some time, but not right then. I let it go for six or seven weeks before I finally made that phone call.

While we were in the hostel, there were travelling people there. One day at the end of February 1992 Ben was minding some of the younger children and one of the travelling women started screaming that Ben had sexually assaulted her little two-year-old girl. She was pulling his hair when I came into the room. He was just standing there crying.

I just saw red and attacked the woman and broke her nose. I didn't mean to hurt her but after everything that Ben had seen, I was livid that someone could accuse my son of doing that. He's not like that, and he hates any sort of violence. If he sees someone hitting someone, Ben just sobs hysterically.

The nuns who were running the place said the other woman had been there longer than me, so I had to leave. I still keep in contact with the nuns and last June, I got a letter from them apologising for the way I'd been treated and saying they'd found out afterwards that Ben hadn't touched the two-year-old girl. The woman had made that story up because she thought I would get a house in Waterford before her. I know they apologised, but I still feel hurt that the nuns didn't believe me at the time.

While I was in Waterford, Agnes came down and we had a chat and I really started to open up to her and tell her little bits of what had been going on. When I moved to Urlingford on 1 March 1992, she came out to see me there. I told her more of what went on and we started to piece it together.

When I was in the flat she came round on three or four occasions and we really got into it. We put dates to it, went through the statement in depth and added more details which I was able to pinpoint.

It was about this time that I met the man who's now my fiancé, Thomas. I had been thumbing a lift into Urlingford with Ben. On the way into town, he asked me if I'd like to go out for a drink with him that night. I said I'd meet him at three o'clock the following afternoon, a Saturday.

We spent an hour in the pub and got on really well together. We started meeting more often and eventually I moved into the same block of flats in Urlingford. Ben and I had our own rooms, and Thomas and I were still just friends.

But then in October 1992, over a cup of tea, Thomas said, "After everything you've been through, would you like to marry me?" I just said yes.

He's a very good and kind man—though he's not very romantic. I got a Valentine card from him this year, but I think that was a sort of miracle!

When I moved to Urlingford, Mammy and Daddy were still at home. Daddy was still drinking, but he was going to Alcoholics Anonymous meetings in Kilkenny. He started that after I left home—but he used to drink the day before he went down to the meetings. Surely, if the man had wanted to give up drink, he'd have gone to the meetings and wouldn't have touched a drop beforehand!

On one occasion, I got my fiancé to drive me up to Loon to see Mammy. I knew she'd be at Loon because at six o'clock she would go and do the jobs. It was always the same pattern. At this time, my father was in hiding, he wouldn't come outside the door. It was my only chance to see Mammy on my own. She couldn't phone me up because Daddy was always in the house.

Mother was in tears up in the haggard. She was absolutely freezing. She had been round and picked bags of blackberries off the ditches for neighbours, as repayment for little things they'd given her. She had no money to pay them back. She was so cold.

I said, "What's wrong with you?" She said, "Yesterday he beat the shit out of me because I wouldn't bring him back a bottle of whiskey. So today I had to bring him back a bottle. I'm afraid to go home." Daddy had passed out on the floor at one o'clock and Mammy had been up at Loon since then. She didn't want to be there when he woke up.

All I wanted to do was take her away, bring her home with me, but she wouldn't come, she just had to stay there.

In May, father went to England. He stayed with his cousin in Bristol for three weeks. Mammy phoned me and said, "He's gone to England, he went yesterday. He phoned me up this morning to let me know he got there OK. Would you like to come up and spend a couple of days with me so I can see how you are?"

I only went up for the day, but at that time the memories of the last beating were so strong that I couldn't stay there any longer.

A month later, Daddy ran away for the second time. Again he went to Bristol. He borrowed £1,000 each time from the bank and used Grandad's name so he wouldn't be found out. The second time he couldn't find the relative he was looking for and his money was pinched from his wallet, so he had to come back.

While he was away, Mammy was to take me down to the hospital in Waterford so I could have treatment on my eye. She came up for me and I stayed the Monday night in the Deerpark. It was the first night I'd spent there since I left home.

At half-past four the following morning, Mammy woke up screaming. She couldn't feel her legs. From the waist down, her legs were blue—just as if you'd broken your hand. Ben was crying, "Mammy, Mammy, what's wrong with you?"

My appointment in Waterford was for a quarter past twelve so Mammy struggled to sit up in bed. "I'm all right," she said, "I'm going to drive you to Waterford."

"You're not," I said, "I'm driving you to the doctor in Carlow."

Now, I've no licence, no insurance, nothing, but I got into the car and drove her to Dr Skuce's in Carlow. He did tests on her and asked her how she got in to him. She said, "I drove." He said, "You're one hell of a woman to drive in here with legs like that. How did you do it?"

He gave her an injection and we left. Outside, I

was going to pull out of the car park, but there were gardai going down in the car. Mammy said, "Hold on for a minute, I can feel the injection working. The pain is going and I can just feel my toes. If you'll hold on for a minute, I'll drive home."

So she drove home. When we got there, I phoned up the place I was staying and the social welfare man and told them where I was staying, why I was there. They said to stay until Mammy didn't need me any more.

I was there a full week with her. She couldn't walk, she couldn't feed the animals, she couldn't even stay on her feet long enough to plug in the kettle or feed herself. I had to stay. I couldn't just leave her the way she was.

In July she went to Waterford Hospital and they put a needle in her hip bone. There wasn't any blood going down to her legs, so they arranged for a bed in Dublin so she could be operated on. During the operation, they cut her from between her breasts, down to her stomach, across and down her thighs. She had two vein grafts and a double bypass because the veins were blocked. The doctors don't know whether it was due to smoking or to the beatings, but they said she was very lucky; if she had been left any longer she would have died.

While Mammy was in Beaumont Hospital, Daddy was in hiding at the house. He'd been phoning her up from England and she told him that he'd have to come back to do the jobs on the farm because she was going into hospital. "Why, what's wrong with you?"

"I'm dying," she said. "Unless I have an operation, the doctors have said I'll die. You'll have to come home and do the jobs." He said there was nothing wrong with her. It sounded like he wanted her to die.

Eventually he did come home but he went into hiding and wouldn't come out of the door. Mammy rang me to say that Keith, a young lad in the Deerpark, had agreed to do the jobs.

One day I paid a fella £2 for diesel to drive me up to Loon. As we passed the house at the Deerpark, I saw Daddy's shadow inside. We got the keys from Keith's mother and went up to Loon to see to the animals.

About a week later, when Mammy was still in the hospital, she told me a neighbour was feeding Daddy. The neighbour was taking Daddy bread, butter, tea bags, milk—just basic stuff to keep him going. Mammy said there should be three health board cheques on the doormat at home. She was getting £53 every second week. She told me to get Daddy to hand over the cheques, sign them and get them changed to pay the neighbour for Daddy's food.

I rang Daddy and told him he had to hand over the cheques. He said, "Where are you?" I said, "They've just let me out to get milk and I have to go back. If I don't go back they'll take Ben away from me." He thought I was in a place in Cork for battered wives.

"Oh, that's OK, pet," he said. "Just mind yourself and we'll all be one happy family again." He expected me to go back home again, and I gave him the impression I wanted to go home and that I wanted to get it all over. That was the only occasion I spoke to him between the time I left home in January 1992 and when he was arrested the following September.

But he still didn't hand over the cheques, so my fiancé took me up to the Deerpark. There were three cheques on the mat. Daddy would read the post, but then he'd put the letters back on the mat so that anyone looking in through the letter box would see them there and think there was nobody in the house.

My fiancé went into the house and told Daddy that Mammy said he was to hand over the cheques. Daddy gave them to him and we took them into 'Comer and cashed them at the supermarket.

All during this period, Daddy was hiding in the bedroom and kitchen. When Mammy got back the stench in the house was unbelievable because he wouldn't flush the toilet in case the people next door would hear him. What he didn't know was that at night when he had the television on, they could hear the telly. He used to have it so low he thought nobody could hear it, but the people next door knew he was in there.

Mammy used to come up and see me in Urlingford while Daddy was hiding in the house. He'd say to her, "You're meeting her. Can't she write a few lines to me?" He was beating Mammy at the time, so I'd write a few lines to try and stop him. Mammy would tell me what he wanted to hear and I'd write it—things like "It'll be all over soon," "Ben's fine, I'll be home soon," or "Don't worry, we'll all be one happy family again." I told the gardai I was sending the letters as protection for my mother, but obviously I didn't mean what I wrote. I just wanted to protect Mammy until the gardai finally arrested Daddy.

1 8

ARREST

Mammy was in hospital for four weeks and Daddy hid in the house all during that time. After she came out of hospital, she went into the garda barracks and made statements against him, but only on the understanding that, until Daddy was charged, the gardai wouldn't say anything about the statements. The gardai eventually came for him one morning in September. Mammy and I had been into the garda station in Kilkenny a couple of days before and I told them, "Mammy can't continue this way. She's sick and, with all the harassment from Daddy, she's only getting worse. She just can't take it."

Superintendent Duffe's words still ring in my ears. He said, "Well, things might be moving sooner than you think." I thought, "Well, it's after taking this long. Nothing's going to happen overnight."

Two days later at five to nine, I was getting Ben

ready for school and a neighbour threw a stone up at the window of my room. "You're wanted on the phone." I thought, "Who wants me at this hour of the morning? Something must be wrong with Mammy."

I went downstairs and it was Mammy on the phone. She was speaking so fast I couldn't understand what she was saying. "Slow down," I said. "What's going on?"

"They came and arrested him this morning," she said, "I've peace at last." She sounded so happy and relieved. "Tell me what happened," I said. "No, I won't tell you over the phone. I'll come down to you. I'll be down in about an hour." I said, "OK, I'll have the kettle on."

When she turned up she told me the whole incident was hilarious.

The morning the gardai arrived, Mammy woke up late. She'd been sleeping in my bedroom and she got up to make coffee. Daddy was still in bed. She turned round and looked out of the window. "Oh, there's a squad car outside the gate."

"Oh Jesus," said Daddy. He pulled on his shirt and underpants. "What are they doing?"

"They're coming up the path," she said. With that, she went to answer the door.

The garda said, "Is Mr Cooper here?"

"No, I'm afraid he's not," said Mammy. She'd told the gardai beforehand that when they came to the door looking for him, she had to say he wasn't there, because he was in the other room listening to her. The gardai knew this and they had a warrant.

"Well, can we search the house?" There were two gardai round the back of the house, two at each window and two going in the front door.

"Well, I don't know," said Mammy. "Have you a warrant?" They said they had, so she let them in.

One garda looked in my room but couldn't see him. They went into the kitchen and through into his room. They looked all round, in the wardrobe, but couldn't find him. All of a sudden Agnes Reddy heard a scratching noise. Now, in under the big double bed, there's a single mattress and what had he done only jammed himself between the mattress and the bottom of the bed!

Agnes said, "Come on out now, Mr Cooper." He said nothing so she pulled at his leg and Mammy said that when they finally got him out, his shirt was up around his shoulders and there was a great big scratch mark along his back where he'd caught it on the bed. Daddy was taken to Abbeyleix court and was remanded to Mountjoy. After a couple more hearings, they finally set a date for the High Court hearing on 28 January. After he pleaded guilty, he was remanded for sentence on 1 March.

Mammy was delighted, absolutely delighted. She'd been looking very old, especially after her operation, but now she looked so much happier, so much better.

While Daddy was in custody, he tried desperately

to blacken my character. He claimed that Ben's father was a man who'd stayed in the house for two or three weeks. This man was a friend of Daddy's who was going through a bad patch in his marriage. But he never touched me. He had enough problems in his own marriage without looking for more trouble.

Recently when Mammy went up to see Daddy in prison, he told her I'd been raped one night by someone at the back of the house. He said she didn't know about it, but he said Tanya and the girl next door knew about it. When Mammy asked them, they said they knew nothing about it. He was trying to throw as much dirt as he could to make me look bad so that he'd look just that little bit better.

Daddy also claimed that when their first baby was burned to death, Mammy had gone off the rails a bit with nerves and had got pregnant with me by another man. Daddy was trying to say that I wasn't his daughter, so the incest charge wouldn't stand up.

He sent a letter to Mammy from Arbour Hill saying, "Mary, please write this out on a separate sheet of paper and give it to your solicitor or mine." He wrote out exactly what he wanted her to say. And, strangely enough, although all the letters from the prison are censored and mailed in franked envelopes, this one came in an ordinary envelope with a stamp on it, so he must have got one of the other prisoners to smuggle it out and post it.

He told other lies too. Just after Grandad died, I

had a chance of a job in England, working in a pub-restaurant. Daddy thought at the time it would be a good idea to keep an eye on Granny after Grandad had died. We thought she could probably do with the company at night.

But Granny didn't want me to come over. She wanted to stay on her own with her memories of how good Grandad was, the times they'd had together. She didn't want anyone spoiling that, so I didn't go over. But Daddy told his solicitor Granny wouldn't have me because I was always out at night drinking with other men. That wasn't true at all, he just wanted to make me look cheap.

When Granny Cooper heard the full news about Daddy, she was absolutely flabbergasted. It's got to the point that she never wants to see her son again. She just said if he ever came near the door, she wouldn't let him in, she'd phone the police and have him arrested.

19

COURT

The first time I saw Daddy after his arrest was in the Central Criminal Court in Dublin on 28 January 1993. The trial was to be in court two in the Four Courts. There were fifty-six charges against Daddy, but he was going to deny everything, bar the actual assault on 16 January 1992.

Agnes had the pornographic photographs but she hadn't handed them round. That morning she gave out copies, and when Daddy saw them, he just pleaded guilty to the six specimen charges. He knew there was no way out.

I'd said all along that I didn't mind Ben having a blood test to prove Daddy was his father, but Agnes said she didn't want to put the child through that unless it was absolutely necessary.

Mammy was there, and my sister Tanya and two friends were with me in one bench. Dinny Dempsey and his son, who were going to give evidence for

Daddy, were in another bench.

Daddy didn't say anything, but at the end of the hearing, he called me over. I stood there and said, "Well?" He didn't say anything. He just started crying and put his arms around my shoulders. I was looking at Mr Matthews and I froze. I couldn't move. It was as if, after my bit of freedom, I was being dumped back into the same situation again. I didn't know what to do, but after a couple of seconds the guy to whom he was handcuffed took him away.

Five weeks later, on 1 March 1993, he was sentenced. They told mother and me we needn't go, but on the day of the hearing they came along and said they wanted mother to be there. But she was minding Ben and, at that short notice, we couldn't get anyone else to mind him. I said, "I don't mind standing up and giving evidence. If that's what's needed, I'll do it."

So nobody came up to the court with me that time except Agnes Reddy. It was such short notice I didn't even have anything to wear; I was wearing my boyfriend's jeans and jumper. I was really only there in case they needed any questions answered.

When I got to the court, I saw him outside, about four benches away, with two prison officers. I didn't look at him after that. He went into the court first and I went in afterwards and sat in the bench behind him.

I was trembling. Agnes said, "Take deep breaths. It'll be all OK. You don't have to worry now. This is the final stepping stone."

We'd only been in the court a few moments when he leaned back to me and said, "Where's your mother?" I said, "Mam can't come because Jess is calving." He said, "You won't have to worry about Loon too much longer," and then turned away. I turned to Superintendent Duffe and he asked, "What's going on?"

"I don't know," I said.

About five or ten minutes later, he turned round again and said to the Superintendent, "Can I speak to her?" Agnes knew I didn't want to speak to him, but the Superintendent said, "Yes, go ahead."

Daddy said to me, "Are you living back at home?"

"Nearly, why?"

"Well, you won't be living there too much longer either."

I was wondering what was going on. Was he going to sell up or what was he going to do? Shortly afterwards, the case was postponed until the afternoon and Daddy kept shaking his head at me, as if to say, "No, you're wrong, you shouldn't have taken it this far." I think he actually believed I was going to give in half-way through and there wouldn't be any court case. He thought he had real power over me and that I wouldn't go through with it.

At two o'clock, when we went back to the court, he was already in the courtroom. It was almost as if I was in another world. I just sat there shaking, wishing it was all over. I wished I could just go to sleep and when I'd wake up, he'd be sentenced and everything would be over. It's as if my body and mind were there, but I was somewhere else.

Daddy didn't speak to me, but he tried passing a letter to Superintendent Duffe, a complaint about Agnes Reddy. But Mr Duffe wouldn't take the letter. He said Daddy would have to post it.

Superintendent Duffe stood up then and gave his evidence and afterwards Agnes stood up and gave hers. At the end of the case, after Daddy had been sentenced, we came out of court first. We were sitting on the bench outside when Daddy came out. We walked down to the lift and Daddy was brought down by the warders. As he passed me, he just said, "Well, kid..." and I could hear him laughing as he was taken down the stairs. It was almost as if he had won.

I went down to the toilets in the restaurant in the Four Courts and I just sat there and cried. I mean, what was it all for? He gets off with six-and-a-half years and just laughs. He thinks he's won and I'm the one who went through everything for nothing.

2 0

THE FUTURE

Now that Daddy is safely in prison—for the time being at least—I can sit down with Mammy and my fiancé and start to think about my own future.

At the moment, I'm working at trying to have a normal relationship with my fiancé. I can hold his hand and I can actually kiss him. One of the blessings I count is that I never kissed my father when he was abusing me and he never made me kiss him. So I find kissing my fiancé very easy. I can let him put his arm around me, but we haven't tried anything more.

I don't even try to think about what sex would be like, not yet. I'm getting counselling and trying to work through it so that I feel comfortable talking about it. At the moment, I don't even feel comfortable discussing it. I just get all shivery inside and feel nervous. I just have to take it one step at a time.

I find there are a lot of men I can't trust—even though I should be able to, because I've known them for a long, long time. If I see a drunken man in a pub, all I want to do now is scream and run. My fiancé sometimes takes me to a pub for a drink and we're trying to work it so that, each time I go to the pub, there are more older men there and I can get used to them.

One time about three weeks ago, one of these men in the pub was very drunk and he came over and put his arm around me. I just froze. I wanted to be out of the situation, but I also knew I had to control it. The man himself didn't know what he was doing, that it was upsetting me. My fiancé was trying to get him to take his arm away without actually saying, "She's been abused, she doesn't like it."

My fiancé was looking at me really worried and I was looking at him and suddenly I thought, "What am I worried about? This man doesn't know what went on, he's not going to attack me, so why am I worried?" The man carried on chatting away. After about ten minutes, I started to relax a little, but I still wasn't exactly comfortable with it.

I can't give a kiss or hug to other men, even uncles or other relatives. My grandmother's brother asked the other day, "When are you coming over to see us?" But I just couldn't even think about it. I know that when I do go over and he meets me off the boat or train, he'll put his arms around me and hug me. I know he won't do me any harm, but I can't face that just yet. Even shaking hands with men, I get nervous.

I'm also trying to rebuild my relationship with my mother. She and I never really had a good time on our own because we couldn't talk about what was going on. We'd chat about things we'd like to do together, places that we'd like to go that we'd never been, buying stuff that we'd never been allowed buy, like perfume, clothes and so on. But we'd never really talk about the abuse.

Mother always had an idea that we'd go to England, to London, and spend a week maybe just looking round the shops, looking to see what other people did. Maybe go to the theatre. I've never actually been to London—the nearest I got was when I went to my aunt's wedding in Sussex.

Now that Daddy's in prison, Mammy's starting to get over her fear of him. She was terrified of him. She's not as strong as I am; she's a very weak person. I can twist her around my little finger now, and I'm not as hard as he was. I really pity her because if she'd been stronger she would have done something years ago. It was just that she was petrified of him.

Before the court case, I never knew if Mammy would stand by me. Even though I know she doesn't love Daddy, I didn't know which way she'd go. It was a chance I didn't really want to take because if I did go to someone and tell my story and then she backed Daddy, I'd look like a liar.

I still haven't managed to discuss all the details of the years of abuse with Mammy. And I'm still not certain why Daddy did what he did. I think one of the reasons he used to abuse me was that he was jealous of me because I was young.

When he began beating Mammy, she wasn't taking care of her appearance. She wouldn't wash her hair or tidy herself up. She wouldn't wear trendy clothes like anyone else's mother. She wasn't really worried about her appearance any more. I wouldn't call myself good-looking, but I was always smartly dressed in jeans and a T-shirt and possibly I reminded him of mother when she was younger.

I don't hate Daddy any longer for what he did to me. I just think he's sick and needs treatment. But I'm hurt and angry that he should have got off so lightly. I know that he'll blame Mammy and me for what has happened to him and that he'll store it up in his mind until he's released. Then he'll come looking for us.

When he gets out, Mammy and I will be looking over our shoulders all the time. I think he should have been given fifteen or twenty years for what he did.

After all, at the end of the day, he'll serve just six-and-a-half years. My sentence is life.